# Decolonial Voices, Lang and Race

## GLOBAL FORUM ON SOUTHERN EPISTEMOLOGIES

*Series Editors:* Sinfree Makoni (*Pennsylvania State University, USA*), Rafael Lomeu Gomes (*University of Oslo, Norway*), Magda Madany-Saá (*Pennsylvania State University, USA*), Bassey E. Antia (*University of the Western Cape, South Africa*) and Chanel Van Der Merwe (*Nelson Mandela University, South Africa*)

This book series publishes independent volumes concerned primarily with exploring peripheralized ways of framing and conducting language studies in both the Global South and Global North. We are particularly interested in the 'geopolitics of knowledge' as it pertains to language studies and aim to illustrate how language scholarship in the Global North is partially indebted to diverse traditions of scholarship in the Global South. We are also keen to explore interfaces between language and other areas of human and non-human scholarship. Ultimately, our concern is not only epistemological; it is also political, educational and social. The books are part of the Global Forum, which is open and politically engaged. The Global Forum fosters collegiality and dialogue, using the technologies essential to productivity during the pandemic that have served our collective benefit. In the book series, we experiment with the format of the book, challenging the colonial concept of a single monologic authorial voice by integrating multiple voices, consistent with decoloniality and the democratic and politically engaged nature of our scholarship.

Full details of all the books in this series and of all our other publications can be found on http://www.multilingual-matters.com, or by writing to Multilingual Matters, St Nicholas House, 31–34 High Street, Bristol, BS1 2AW, UK.

GLOBAL FORUM ON SOUTHERN EPISTEMOLOGIES: 1

# Decolonial Voices, Language and Race

Edited by
**Sinfree Makoni,
Magda Madany-Saá,
Bassey E. Antia and
Rafael Lomeu Gomes**

MULTILINGUAL MATTERS
Bristol • Jackson

*This volume one is dedicated to*
*Johey Tonny Verfaille.*

DOI https://doi.org/10.21832/MAKONI3481
Library of Congress Cataloging in Publication Data
A catalog record for this book is available from the Library of Congress.
Names: Makoni, Sinfree, editor. | Madany-Saá, Magda, editor. |
  Antia, Bassey Edem, editor. | Gomes, Rafael Lomeu, editor.
Title: Decolonial Voices, Language and Race/Edited by Sinfree Makoni,
  Magda Madany-Saá, Bassey E. Antia and Rafael Lomeu Gomes.
Description: Bristol; Jackson: Multilingual Matters, [2022] |
  Series: Global Forum on Southern Epistemologies: 1 | Includes bibliographical
  references and index. | Summary: "This groundbreaking book echoes the
  growing demand for decolonization of the production and dissemination of
  academic knowledge. Reflecting the dynamic nature of online discussion,
  this conversational book features interviews with scholars working on
  language and race and the interactive discussion that accompanied these
  interviews"— Provided by publisher.
Identifiers: LCCN 2022003267 (print) | LCCN 2022003268 (ebook) | ISBN
  9781800413481 (hardback) | ISBN 9781800413474 (paperback) | ISBN
  9781800413504 (epub) | ISBN 9781800413498 (pdf)
Subjects: LCSH: Sociolinguistics. | Decolonization. | Education,
  Higher—Social aspects. | Racism in higher education. | Developing
  countries—Intellectual life. | Developing
  countries—Relations—Developed countries. | Developed
  countries—Relations—Developing countries.
Classification: LCC P40 .D34 2022 (print) | LCC P40 (ebook) | DDC
  306.44—dc23/eng/20220420
LC record available at https://lccn.loc.gov/2022003267
LC ebook record available at https://lccn.loc.gov/2022003268

British Library Cataloguing in Publication Data
A catalogue entry for this book is available from the British Library.

ISBN-13: 978-1-80041-348-1 (hbk)
ISBN-13: 978-1-80041-347-4 (pbk)

**Multilingual Matters**
UK: St Nicholas House, 31–34 High Street, Bristol, BS1 2AW, UK.
USA: Ingram, Jackson, TN, USA.

Website: www.multilingual-matters.com
Twitter: Multi_Ling_Mat
Facebook: https://www.facebook.com/multilingualmatters
Blog: www.channelviewpublications.wordpress.com

The policy of Multilingual Matters/Channel View Publications is to use papers that are natural, renewable
and recyclable products, made from wood grown in sustainable forests. In the manufacturing process of
our books, and to further support our policy, preference is given to printers that have FSC and PEFC Chain
of Custody certification. The FSC and/or PEFC logos will appear on those books where full certification
has been granted to the printer concerned.

Typeset by Nova Techset Private Limited, Bengaluru and Chennai, India.
Printed and bound in the UK by the CPI Books Group Ltd.

# Contents

Acknowledgements       vii
Foreword       ix

Introduction       1
*Sinfree Makoni, Magda Madany-Saá, Bassey E. Antia and
    Rafael Lomeu Gomes*

1   Language and Decolonization in Institutions of Higher
    Learning in Africa       13
    *Kwesi Kwaa Prah*

2   Linguistics, Race and Fascism       24
    *Christopher Hutton*

3   Struggle, Voice, Justice: A Conversation and Some Words of Caution
    about the Sociolinguistics We Hope For       48
    *Monica Heller and Bonnie McElhinny*

4   Black Bodies       68
    *Robbie Shilliam*

5   Linguistics for Legal Purposes       84
    *John Baugh*

Epilogue: Transcending Metonymic Reason: Foregrounding
Southern Coordinates of Sociolinguistic Thought and Rethinking
Academic Cultures       98
*Bassey E. Antia*

Index       110

# Acknowledgements

I would like to take this opportunity to acknowledge the many people who have worked with me in various capacities in the African Studies Global Virtual Forum. First, thank you to those who were engaged in the early reading group, which provided the basis for the Forum's formation: Sibusiso Ndlangamandhla, Anna Kaiper-Marquez, Desmond Odugu, Rafael Lomeu Gomes, Alastair Pennycook and Magdalena Madany-Saá. Some of these individuals – along with Bassey Antia, Kim Hansen, Chanel van der Merwe and Visnja Milojicic – continue to play an active role in shaping the nature of the Forum. I would also like to express my gratitude to Cristine Severo and Ashraf Abdelhay for consistently advertising the Forum through their listserv, Literacy and Applied Linguistics in Africa.

I would like to thank all the guest speakers who graciously agreed to share their knowledge with us in the Forum. Without their engagement, it would not have been possible to have the Forum and, subsequently, the book series. My thanks go especially to those speakers whose work is included in this volume: Kwesi Kwaa Prah, Christopher Hutton, Monica Heller and Bonnie McElhinny, Robbie Shilliam and John Baugh. I thank all the Forum's global participants who took the time to listen together and contribute to the conversation. Rafael Lomeu Gomes would like to thank Zahir Athari for assisting with the transcription of Heller and McElhinny's session. Thanks, too, to our publishers, Multilingual Matters, for their vision and faith in us.

I thank Johey Tonny Verfaille, the events organizer for the Program of African Studies, who is the Forum's administrative linchpin. Her efficient dedication has been the force behind her informative emails, her creative flyers and her unfailing responses to members' queries. I would like to thank Anisa Caine for the numerous enriching conversations that I had with her before and after each session, and also for designing the book's cover. Our editorial team, composed of Alastair Pennycook, John Joseph, Jason Litzenberg, Oyeronke Oyewumi, Busi Makoni and Jane Gordon, are deserving of thanks for generously giving their time and invaluable feedback.

I'm grateful to Busi Makoni for the multiple roles she has played in this Forum as interlocutor and dependable supporter.

Finally, my thanks to Clarence Lang, the Dean of the College of Liberal Arts, Penn State University, who provided the funding to transcribe the material.

With my deep gratitude
*Sinfree Makoni*

# Foreword

Reflecting on changes to academic life over the last decade, shortly before his death in early 2021, Jan Blommaert (2020) bemoaned the 'academic industrial culture' that had developed during his career. He was saddened by the individualisation of academic work, the incessant performance measurement, the emphasis on competition, which was pushing colleagues to stressful extremes and to invest in work at the expense of other aspects of life, a celebrity culture of rock-star plenary speakers (he had, to his chagrin, allowed himself to become one, as he admitted), while underpaid, casualised academics used whatever resources they had to attend conferences and get a foot on the slippery academic ladder. As Connell (2019) similarly notes, growing distrust between dwindling staff and autocratic managers, the increase in internal regulation of teaching and workloads, the commodification of research findings, the casualisation of labour, and the hunt for short-term gain by the enterprise university have all undermined an older culture of collegiality and the knowledge common.

This new culture, Blommaert continued, 'took away and delegitimized a previous culture, one of collegial dialogue, collaboration, slowness, time to think, to reflect and to doubt, periods of invisibility and absence from public stages – because one was doing some serious bit of research, for instance'. And yet, it is worth reminding ourselves that this perhaps rather rosy-eyed view of an academic past when we talked and collaborated, and took our time to reflect, was never an inclusive collegiality. The collaboration was still only between those who could join the club. If in the current era of expensive international conferences, underpaid and underfunded casual academics must borrow money to join the jamboree, there has always been a much larger population for whom this was never even going to be an option. The cost of travel and accommodation, the price of conferences, the difficulty of getting visas, the systemic racism that excluded many from the chance to speak, meant they had never been able to go in the first place. This is why this project, of which this book is an essential part, has been so very important.

Not much good has come out of the global COVID-19 pandemic. We would not expect it to. The catchcry of the pandemic – 'We're all in this together' – urging the world to act together, turned out, of course, to obscure the deep inequalities the pandemic exposed. While the wealthy and the white-collared could stay at home to work, many others lost their jobs; the well-off self-isolated in their holiday homes; the poor were incarcerated in crowded apartment blocks. Many old people died, often alone, and their families couldn't attend their funerals. It cast a harsh light on multiple forms of inequality: women's work was hardest hit because of the deep-seated inequities of employment, especially casual employment, and particularly in service industries; working class, migrants and communities of colour suffered much more than their wealthy White neighbours because of closer living conditions, work in frontline industries with greater exposure to the virus, job losses, the use of public transport and reliance on other public facilities, and limited access to digital resources or health services.

Amid all the panic, the pandemic spotlighted these continuing forms of inequality, as issues of race, gender, class, housing, unemployment and health intersected. Frontline health workers received praise in some quarters, but were vilified in others for becoming too tired or scared to continue their work, for doing double shifts across different hospitals (and why did they need to do so?). Other workers, such as security guards, were taken to task for having risky second jobs (why were they doing pizza delivery at the weekends?) and even, it seemed, for coming from large, inter-generational families. Random racist attacks on Asians increased as shameful dog-whistling about the 'China virus' stirred up already disillusioned and racist publics. It is never a good time to be ruled by authoritarian, xenophobic, misogynist leaders, but the pandemic was a particularly bad time. Communal action, social health care, wearing face masks (politicized in some countries) were anathema to conservative leaders, and many thousands of people have paid for this with their lives. Meanwhile, as the wealthy countries hoarded their precious vaccines, the Global South was once again left to struggle on its own.

During this grim time, it was therefore a pleasure to have something more positive to look forward to. The Forum on which this book is based defied these trends – exclusionary academic and limited pandemic interactions – opening up an online dialogue between North and South, and at least equally importantly, across the South. It was free and open and politically engaged. It fostered collegiality and dialogue. And it was able to use the technologies we had been forced into (our new Zoom-world) to its advantage. This volume generally reflects the middle stage (there are more volumes on the way) of this project – between the early small-group discussions of books and the later talks by authors – that sought to challenge and decentre Western canons of knowledge in order to open a space for other ways of knowing.

Such a project requires several things: firstly, global participation, where 'global' means not so much lots of people from around the world, but rather many loci of enunciation – not just where people are speaking but the geographical, historical, bodily and ideological contexts from which positions are articulated (Figueiredo & Martinez, 2021). Secondly, a broad program that defies disciplinary confines: there is a focus on language across these chapters, but several of the speakers come from non-linguistic backgrounds, and the topics range from higher education in Africa, or racist and fascist influences on linguistics, to the absence of Black women's bodies in sociolinguistics or White public and imperial spaces, and ways to oppose raciolinguistic profiling – a broad political agenda that has decolonization at its heart. As Mufwene (2020: 290) suggests, *decolonial linguistics* 'entails reducing the Western bias and hegemony in how languages of the global South and the (socio) linguistic behaviours of their speakers and writers are analysed'. Thirdly, a willingness to listen, to discuss, to understand, to work out what is being said and why, how this might be responded to, and an interest in talking through the issues on the table.

This all started – if we are to accept the narrative provided by the editors of this book – with a suggestion when Rafael Lomeu was visiting me in Sydney, that it might be useful to have a three-way conversation (using Skype – remember that?) with Sinfree Makoni, since he and I were also discussing the new Mignolo and Walsh (2018) book. Makoni and I had just started work on our new joint venture (Pennycook & Makoni, 2020) and had a long reading list we wanted to discuss. When I moved to New York for a semester in 2018 (to work with Ofeila García and others) we continued, with Lynn Mario Menezes de Sousa in São Paulo and Sibusiso Cliff Ndlangamandla in South Africa joining in. This may indeed be a plausible account of its beginnings, but it really took off in 2020 (I had little involvement, caught up with family bereavements and cornered by the inconvenience of time zones). But we perhaps need to get better at telling more polycentric and polychronic stories than this kind of origin myth. While Makoni was the linchpin throughout (supported at Penn State by Valeriya Minakova, Magda Madany-Saá and Johey Verfaille), and of course Busi Makoni and others joined in and took the reins – Rafael, by then back in Oslo, and Desmond Odugu and Bassey Antia – it is important to view the evolution of such a forum as starting in many places, at different times, with diverse interests. In many ways, it is the participants who made it.

This edited volume, then, is to be welcomed for many reasons. It is dialogic in a more meaningful sense than some texts that, like celebrity interviews, pose questions designed to allow for long expositions. Here there is discussion, interruption, disagreement. A textual rendering of these discussions unfortunately only reveals part of the dynamics of such online debates. It is political in ways that do more than just expound an obvious ideological position: if decoloniality and race are the constant themes that cut across all discussions, there is much more going on in terms of how we understand hope, place, local knowledge, elite knowledge, forms of universalism, citation practices, water, statues, and trying to rent apartments (from Wole Soyinka's poem in 1963 until today, not much has changed). And it is significant in terms of the questions it asks about decolonization: what does this mean in relation to universities in Africa, linguistics as commonly practised, Indigenous ways of knowing, public space, legal processes? This book shows what is possible, despite North–South disparities and global lockdowns, and it promises much for the future.

*Alastair Pennycook*
University of Technology Sydney

## References

Blommaert, J. (2020) Looking back: What was important? https://alternative-democracy-research.org/2020/04/20/what-was-important/

Connell, R. (2019) *The Good University: What Universities Actually Do and Why It's Time for Radical Change*. London: Zed Books.

Figueiredo, E.H.D. and Martinez, J. (2021) The locus of enunciation as a way to confront epistemological racism and decolonize scholarly knowledge. *Applied Linguistics* 42 (2), 355–359.

Mignolo, W. and Walsh, C. (2018) *On Decoloniality: Concepts, Analytics, Praxis*. Durham, NC: Duke University Press.

Mufwene, S. (2020) Decolonial linguistics as paradigm shift: A commentary. In A. Deumert, A. Storch and N. Shepherd (eds) *Colonial and Decolonial Linguistics: Knowledges and Epistemes* (pp. 289–300). Oxford: Oxford University Press.

Pennycook, A. and Makoni, S. (2020) *Innovations and Challenges in Applied Linguistics from the Global South*. London: Routledge.

# Introduction

Sinfree Makoni, Magda Madany-Saá,
Bassey E. Antia and Rafael Lomeu Gomes

This volume, the first in a series, has arisen from a lively and profoundly productive set of initial engagements in the African Studies Global Forum (ASGF) led by Sinfree Makoni at the Pennsylvania State University, USA. Incidentally, the ASGF has two origins. It began in February/March 2020 as a virtual reading group centered on the kitchen table of the Makoni household in State College in Pennsylvania. An initial group of Desmond Odugu, Sinfree Makoni, Sibusiso Ndlangamandla, Anna Kaiper-Marquez, Magdalena Madany-Saá, Lynn Mario Menezes de Souza and Alastair Pennycook met regularly to discuss a number of books. At about the same time as these kitchen table sessions were going on, Alastair Pennycook was also reading some texts (e.g. Mignolo & Walsh's 2018 book *On Decoloniality*) with Rafael Lomeu Gomes, who had been visiting Alastair's University of Technology Sydney, Australia, as part of his PhD. Alastair saw merit in having the Sydney Forum join the State College ASGF group.

Africa only lends its name to the forum because the latter is run from the African Studies Program at the Pennsylvania State University, and not because of any exclusive intellectual focus on Africa. The shape of the ASGF changed after the group had discussed the following books:

Ingold, T. (2015) *The Life of Lines*. London: Routledge.

Kohn, E. (2013) *How Forests Think: Toward an Anthropology beyond the Human*. Berkeley: University of California Press.

Descola, P. (2013) *Beyond Nature and Culture* (J. Lloyd, trans.). Chicago: University of Chicago Press.

Heller, M. and McElhinny, B. (2017) *Language, Capitalism, Colonialism: Toward a Critical History*. Toronto: University of Toronto Press.

It was decided that, instead of just in-group interaction, there was merit in drawing in the authors of books into the conversations. This decision turned out to have several consequences. The ASGF was no longer a small group meeting – attendance sometimes reached 250 participants from all over the world. A host of organizational decisions had to be taken, including technological support, publicity, identifying and contacting authors, moderation of the sessions. Fortunately, the goodwill of a number of people across the world as well as a series of events all conspired to place the enlarged Forum on a sound footing. Johey Verfaille, the event organizer for the

Program of African Studies at Pennsylvania State University, gracefully took on responsibility for creating membership lists, distributing announcements, preparing flyers for each session, and managing the supporting technology. Cristine Severo (in Brazil) placed at the service of ASGF the listserv for the Research Network Africa (REN), which she and Ashraf Abdelhay (in Qatar) jointly manage, a research network that was previously part of the International Association of Applied Linguistics (AILA). Bassey Antia (in South Africa), who was spending part of his sabbatical leave with Sinfree Makoni, took on organizational responsibilities.

Several other ideological positions had to be clarified. Philosophically, there was commitment to the idea that 'all knowledges are socio-historically situated and local and that there are inextricable connections between colonialism, patriarchy and capitalism' (de Souza, 2022: forthcoming; see also de Sousa Santos, 2016). Also, we deliberately chose a policy of free membership and access to the ASGF so that, in our own small but significant way, we could challenge inequalities in access to knowledge production between the Global North and Global South. Many conferences, even online, continue to be expensive.

As a consequence of these measures, the current membership of the ASGF is diverse geographically (Africa, Asia, Australia, Europe, North America and South America) and in terms of professional status (activists, artists and academics at different career stages, from graduate students to retired professors). Similarly, presenters at the ASGF situate themselves in, but more often across, disciplines such as Linguistics, Sociology, Political Science, African Studies, Anthropology, Literature, Development Studies, Cultural Studies, Gender Studies, Higher Education Studies, among others. They are all united by a common quest for alternative ways of framing contemporary academic and social challenges.

The reception accorded to the ASGF has been so overwhelming that the initial idea to have monthly or at most fortnightly sessions has had to give way to practically weekly meetings. At the time of writing, slots have been booked for the next fourteen months. The phenomenal expansion of the Forum has also seen an expansion in the team micro-managing the sessions: Johey Verfaille, Rafael Lomeu Gomes, Sinfree Makoni, Visnja Milojicic, Chanel van der Merwe, Magdalena Madany-Saá, Kim Hansen and Bassey Antia.

There are pre-reading tasks for each meeting of the Forum. Announcements encourage would-be participants at a particular meeting to familiarize themselves with relevant published works of the speaker. To illustrate, for sessions that make up this inaugural volume, participants were expected to have familiarized themselves with the 2018 *The Challenge of Decolonizing Education* (for the Kwesi Prah session); the 1999 *Linguistics and the Third Reich: Mother-tongue Fascism* (for the Christopher Hutton session); the 2017 *Language, Capitalism, Colonialism: Toward a Critical History* (co-authored by Monica Heller and Bonnie McElhinny for their joint session); the 2019 article, 'Behind the Rhodes statue: Black competency and the imperial academy' (for the Robbie Shilliam session); and the 2018 *Linguistics in Pursuit of Justice* (for the John Baugh session).

What was the global context into which the ASGF was inserting itself? Among others, there was: (a) the 2015 #RhodesMustFall and #FeesMustFall events that initially took place in South Africa and subsequently spread to European and North American universities; (b) Black Lives Matter, (c) the #MeToo movement, (d) the COVID-19 pandemic, and (e) the (continuing) crisis associated with responding to the needs of displaced persons. Even though these movements were global, individuals in local contexts reacted to them in ways that varied substantially. Living in different regions of the globe, members of the ASGF were understandably being impacted differently by the same global events. One only has to consider the spectrum of state and other responses to the COVID-19 pandemic or the case for real inclusion of diversity in universities.

The call to decolonize universities in South Africa is understood as part of a wider anti-colonial movement (Bhambra *et al.*, 2018). The South African students' #FeesMustFall movement highlighted the urgency of decolonization, a theme that Kwesi Prah and Robbie Shilliam address in their respective chapters in this volume. The call for decolonization in European and North American universities was, in part, triggered by the #RhodesMustFall and #FeesMustFall movements in South Africa. Even though decoloniality takes place across different geopolitical spaces and disciplines, it does not have uniform characteristics. The call for decolonization in the United Kingdom, particularly England, is, according to Comaroff (2022), substantially different from the one playing itself out in North America especially in respect of what is meant by colonization and how it should be understood in geospatial and political-theoretical terms. In 'settler colonies' (Mamdani, 2020), such as the United States, decolonization is frequently used as a metaphor, a shorthand, a proxy for struggles of social justice. Decolonization has also been an issue in Eastern European countries that did not have the direct experience of colonialism because state socialism, according to Karkov (2015), is incomplete decolonization. Suárez-Krabbe (2021) argues that it is not only the formerly colonized who need to be decolonized: White Denmark also needs decolonization.

In a reflection of what Mogstad and Tse (2018) refer to as 'the old margins' constituting 'the new frontiers', we see here how events in the Global South set in motion a series of events in the Global North. This rarely acknowledged idea of how the Global South may lead the Global North, or how events in the South may provide insight into events in the Global North, is one that Comaroff and Comaroff (2011) capture in *Theory from the South: Or, How Euro-America is Evolving towards Africa*. That is, Africa provides a conceptual model not only on how to analyze late modern life, but on how to build analytical templates which enable us to think through the impasse of political modernity (Mamdani, 2020).

Through its speakers, the ASGF is committed to supporting the cause of 'building an alternative normative' in response to a prevailing Northern epistemological orthodoxy. In advancing decolonization as a rejoinder to this orthodoxy, the Forum is not unaware of critiques of the decolonial lens. Scholars such as Achille Mbembe have questioned the effectiveness of the call for decolonization because they feel that universities have undergone radical change that incorporated decolonization, with the implication that the call for decolonization may be misplaced. The African historian, Paul Zeleza, argues that decolonization paradoxically enhances the importance of Eurocentricism by overlooking alternative sources of knowledge, which did not originate in Europe, that permeate Africa. Taiwo (2019: 135) argues that, at least in African philosophy, and, in particular, in the work of Ngugi wa Thiong'o and Ghanaian philosopher, Kwasi Wiredu:

> the viability of the conceptualization of decolonization in philosophy may have been oversold; the trope may give false impression of the complexity of the situation it is designed to help attenuate, it may have deleterious consequences on discourse and its progress even if they are unintended.

The broader application of the term *decolonization* has been vehemently opposed by Tuck and Yang (2012), who are adamant that the term should be restricted to its narrow meaning of repatriation of Indigenous land and life; otherwise, it loses its original meaning and becomes an 'empty signifier'.

With respect to disciplines, decolonization may mean different things, but the core of diverse projects is to challenge the 'Eurocentricism and white male hetero-normative foundations as well as attitudes, institutional order and day-to-day prac-tices that allow Eurocentricism and white male heteronormativity to dominate the discipline' (Maldonado-Torres *et al.*, 2018: 65).

Apart from the decolonial air of the times, the ASGF was also birthed in the #MeToo era, which can be construed as an awareness of gender-based violence that destroys the well-being, lives and health of millions of women and the vulnerable across different regions of the world (Chandra & Erlingsdottir, 2021). #MeToo also can be construed as part of the continuing history of resistance of Black women and marginalized women. The movement adopted decolonial, antiracist, non-binary and ecological perspectives as ways of resisting neoliberal, capitalist, market-oriented support of patriarchy. 'It is as well to note, when judging the achievements of the #MeToo movement, that there are no comparable historical examples of social rec-ognition and awareness of sexual discrimination on this global scale' (Chandra & Erlingsdottir, 2021: 7).

The #MeToo movement has been successful in bringing about cross-sectional and intergenerational platforms. The impact of the #MeToo movement has been varied and uneven. In China #RiceBunny, #AnYeYiYang and #WoYeShi were established to sidestep censorship, while in Romania, the #MeToo movement delib-erately cooperated with the police and the Romanian regime (Chandra & Erlingsdottir, 2021).

It was in the #MeToo climate that difficult questions about the appropriateness of citing the research of scholars accused of being sexually predatory, such as the powerful sociolinguist Dell Hymes, were discussed. The allegations of Dell Hymes's sexually predatory behavior were reported by Heller and McElhinny (2017).

An important spinoff of #MeToo was how discussions of sexual predatoriness morphed into investigations into Black women's intellectual activism. The discussions about Black women's academic activism are not about the degree to which these scholars are included but, rather, the extent to which their presence can reshape the nature of mainstream scholarship (Bhambra & Holmwood, 2021; Makoni, 2021).

The ASGF also had its origins in a political climate shaped by Black Lives Matter, which was a movement that emerged in the United States after the killing of Trayvon

Martin in 2012 by George Zimmerman. It drew attention to police brutality against Black men and women in the United States. Within the Black Lives Matter movement, Blackness is a spectrum of vision. According to Ekotto (2021), and Gordon (2022), the spectrum of Blackness includes not only Blacks in Africa, but Afro-Argentinians, Afro-Brazilians and people of African descent. The term *Global Blackness* is also used by Indigenous movements that may not have any African origins but are adopting political strategies popularized by African movements. Further, the notion of Global Blackness is used analytically by Jane Gordon as a way of framing the Global South. The killing of George Floyd in 2020 at the hands of the police provoked an international protest movement in the United States and across the globe, in which protesters of different races and generations participated. The protest movements also occurred across the globe in cities such as Accra, Nairobi, London and Amsterdam. Overall, the Black Lives Matter movement demanded Black dignity. The objectives of the movement were articulated by Alicia Garza, co-founder of Black Lives Matter, and cited in Ekotto (2021):

How do we live in a world that dehumanizes and still be human

The fight is not just being able to keep breathing as a human.

The fight is actually to be able to walk down the street with your head held high –

and feel like I belong here,

or I have right to a level of dignity

The pandemic brought attention and poignancy to police brutality against Black youth and brought to the surface issues about racial inequality and mass incarceration of these youth. Black Lives Matter, like #MeToo, assumed diverse forms across the globe. It drew attention to the long history of violence against Black people, going back to slavery, colonialism and apartheid, as manifesting in police brutality. Black Lives Matter is part of an ongoing struggle against White supremacy, and the ASGF can be construed as part of the ongoing struggle against academic White supremacy.

In Australia, Black Lives Matter brought to the fore the deaths of Indigenous peoples in prisons, underscoring discussions about Indigeneity. In Bulgaria, Black Lives Matter brought attention to anti-Black racism, even in contexts in which there were very few Blacks (cf. Karkov, 2015). In Nigeria, Black Lives Matter offered an ideological and organizational model for local protests such as the 2020 #EndSARS protests against police brutality and the dehumanizing of citizens. Discussions about race were taking place in contexts in which there was a powerful tendency to frame Blackness less in terms of situationally specific Blackness and more in terms of Global Blackness.

Another important set of global events that provided the bigger context in which the ASGF was taking place was the COVID-19 pandemic. According to Diagne (2021), the pandemic triggered what he calls *tribalisms and populisms*. The tribalisms were evident in the emergence of powerful anti-Asian racisms. In contrast to the increasing discrimination, there was also the emergence of powerful multilateral responses to the pandemic, which Diagne argues is encapsulated in the argument by Dr Anthony Fauci that the best way of handling the global pandemic is to give the Global South the capability to produce their own vaccines. When the pandemic initially occurred, there was widespread prediction that Africa, due to its weak health infrastructure, would face devastating consequences. Fortunately, for reasons that Diagne argues are not yet fully known, this did not occur.

In its challenge of canons and bid to mainstream 'alternative normatives', the ASGF goes one step further than comparable initiatives by also seeking to challenge the notion of the 'book'. It implements alternative ways in which books may be put together, including chats in chapters and blending together genres, producing what we call 'conversational chapters'. Decolonization of the book is necessary because it is difficult to envisage how decolonization of disciplines can occur if the idea of a book, which underpins the production of knowledge, remains unchallenged. The notion of a book has remained largely unchanged since the emergence of the printing press.

The genre of a 'talking book' or 'conversational book' is not new. As Ira Shor (2017) recalls, Paulo Freire coined the term 'talking book' in the 1980s and, in fact, prior to his first talking book *A Pedagogy for Liberation* (Shor & Freire, 1987). In that book, Ira and Paulo maintain a 'dialogue about a dialogue', engaging in discussion about the intersection of race, class and sex in achieving a liberating or transformative education. Freire continued with the tradition of a talking book; in 1990, he published the edited transcripts of his conversation with Miles Horton in *We Make the Road by Walking*. One of the reasons Freire insisted on a talking book with Horton was because he wanted to show an American audience that Horton, who lived in the so-called 'first world', had similar educational challenges and solutions to Freire's for the 'third world' (Horton & Freire, 1990).

This volume and subsequent ones will be in the tradition of 'talking books'; they can be seen as collections of 'conversational chapters'. For this volume, the automated transcripts of proceedings were reviewed carefully. We used our discretion to delete repetitions, or aspects of informal conversations which would render reading more difficult. We intervened to address incomplete sentence fragments, repetitions, mis-transcriptions. Many of these were done in consultation with speakers at the various sessions and had relatively limited effect on the conversational character of the chapters. Some speakers substantially rewrote segments of their conversational chapters, clarifying issues and providing further details.

As editors of this volume and co-organizers of the ASGF, we have come to the decolonial table shaped by different experiences, which we document in the following personal vignettes.

### Sinfree Makoni

I am a Black male migrant who is interested in the sociolinguistics of African languages at a major, yet rural, university in the Global North. I, however, continue to retain strong personal and professional ties with many institutions in the Global South. If I had not been a nomadic scholar, I would not have developed a strong interest in how knowledges are produced, developed and circulated across the globe. The fact that I am working on African sociolinguistics, a topic of marginal interest, has created and led to feelings of double marginalization for me. The advantages of the marginality have led me to develop a sharper sense of Eurocentrism and the centrality of the American empire in sociolinguistics. My personal history as a scholar, who has a racialized history, adds another important wrinkle to my academic life interest in race. This has led me to an interest in colonial linguistics, Black Linguistics, discrimination and Epistemologies of the South. I'm particularly interested in exploring how sociolinguistics would look like if it were framed from the Global South. I argue that, philosophically, some of the ideas which are important in contemporary sociolinguistics such as multilingualism and ontology were already in circulation in Africa prior to their appearance in the Global North. Conceptually, I argue that modern sociolinguistics is moving and gravitating towards African sociolinguistics.

When I grew up, I did not draw and maintain any firmer distinctions between human and non-humans. The sociolinguistics which I seek to develop is one that goes beyond the human and includes communication with other species. This is a transdisciplinary approach which transcends the boundaries of single disciplines. Inasmuch as no single country can adequately and fully contain my research, my interests cannot be contained within one discipline.

## Magda Madany-Saá

There is a place in Ecuador, outside of the capital of Quito, called 'La Mitad del Mundo' (The Middle of the World) where one can physically stand on the invisible line of zero latitude. My embodied experience on the equator with one foot in the northern hemisphere and the other in the southern hemisphere inspired me to reflect on my entanglements and consequent positioning. I'm writing this piece sitting on my yellow sofa in a comfortable house that I own, enjoying my life in the lovely and safe university town of State College, Pennsylvania, USA. One foot is located not only in the northern hemisphere but in the Global North, in the nest of modernity, capitalism and ongoing coloniality. My other foot is located in the southern hemisphere, where I interpret my current situation as the place where Indigenous peoples were removed, violently displaced and their lands were stolen under a deceitful figure of treaties. The university where I have the privilege to pursue doctoral studies, The Pennsylvania State University, has several campuses that are located on the original homelands of the Erie, Haudenosaunee (Seneca, Cayuga, Onondaga, Oneida, Mohawk and Tuscarora), Lenni Lenape: Unalachtigo, Unami and Munsee (Delaware), Shawnee (Absentee, Eastern and Oklahoma), Susquehannock and Wahzhazhe (Osage) Nations.

I realize my entanglements between the Global North and the Global South expand beyond my current life and location. My autoethnography reinvents my voice as a researcher embracing experiences from both the Global North and the Global South. I am simultaneously heir of Kościuszko's insurrection for independence of Poland, a personification of Malinche and Hernán Cortes' relationship in the so-called 'New World', and a green card holder of the 'American dream'. Born in communist Poland, I later emigrated to Ecuador, where I started my Polish-Ecuadorian family. After more than a decade of living in middle-class Quito, I found myself painfully awaiting stability in the liminal space of conditioned visa holders in Trump's America First. My mobility and entanglement in diverse dimensions of unequal power relations are not blind spots in decolonizing scholarship but rather vehicles for critical self-reflection on where one's feet are located.

## Rafael Lomeu Gomes

My engagement with the project that has led to the editing of this volume is shaped by my over 10-year professional experience in Teaching English to Speakers of Other Languages in Brazil, and my international and transdisciplinary academic background in social sciences (Pontifícia Universidade Católica de São Paulo, Brazil), linguistics (Queen Mary, University of London, UK) and sociolinguistics (University of Oslo, Norway).

Having lived most of my life in the Global South and being academically socialized in higher education institutions in the Global North, three notions have helped me to make sense of the intersecting space that I inhabit. Anzaldúa (1987: i), for example, conceptualizes the border not only in its physical dimension, but also in its psychological, sexual and spiritual dimensions, which are present 'wherever two or more cultures edge each other, where people of different races occupy the same territory, where under, lower, middle and upper classes touch, where the space between two individuals shrinks with intimacy'. To inhabit this border, according to Anzaldúa, implies embracing identities as multiple and dynamic, and conceiving of power struggles as traversed by axes of social class, race/ethnicity and gender/sexuality. In turn, Pratt (1991: 34), proposes *contact zones* as 'social spaces where cultures meet, clash, and grapple with each other, often in contexts of highly asymmetrical relations of power, such as colonialism, slavery, or their aftermaths as they are lived out in many parts of the world today'. Finally, Cusicanqui (2019: 117) draws on the notion of *ch'ixi*, for it 'reflects the Aymara idea of something that is and is not at the same time. It is the logic of the included third'.

As noted, the notions above have been crucial in my attempts to better understand the entanglements between my locus of enunciation and my academic work. This reflection has been furthered in a recent ethnographically oriented, sociolinguistic project where I analyzed the extent to which language practices in everyday interactions in the home of Brazilian-Norwegian families living in Norway were informed by broader language ideologies (Lomeu Gomes, 2021). Participating in the Virtual Forum has played an important role in the development of this sociolinguistic project. That is, the engagement with concepts and perspectives proposed by many of our guest speakers allowed me to frame analyses of the participants' South-North migration trajectories and their localized linguistic practices with the robust body of works stemming from discussions around decoloniality, epistemologies of the south, and southern theory.

## Bassey Antia

Co-hosting Sinfree's Virtual Forum series, convening a conference on de/coloniality, working on a number of projects pivoting around language and knowledge in the Global Southern experience – these are some of the activities I am engaged in as I write. A life-long archive of misrecognition, microaggression, power inequalities, experienced in my peripatetic trajectory across the globe, would seem to have primed me for these activities. With Sinfree and our numerous collaborators around the world, I am on a journey of sense-making. I seek to understand, but also to push back on, the psychology of colonialism. This is no doubt a tall order. My quest is about connecting the phenomenological dots and understanding how systemic the subaltern experience is across the Global South. To be clear, it is as much about understanding subtle forms of domination as it is about the *epidermalization of inferiority* – by which Fanon (1986) means the fact of persons of color constantly relativizing themselves to Whiteness. I am particularly drawn to misrecognition and microaggression in language and in the academy.

How do I forget being told to take Africa out from the title of a submitted book manuscript because the book won't sell, because potential readers won't understand the examples? Yet, it should be no problem for the African child to read about Hamelin, Grenoble or Guildford in their primer. How do I forget being told by a reviewer that my manuscript needed extensive language editing when the reviewer's own text was strewn with linguistic land mines? The *a priori* assumption of course was that I was African and a non-native and irremediably incompetent user of English. How do I forget when it was, let's just say, rumored that a *summa cum laude*, the highest distinction in the particular institutional context, was reserved for the brightest of national students, not for their international peers in whose home countries such a distinction would in any case be meaningless?

How do I forget being asked at a conference in Cologne: *Wie fühlen Sie sich als der einzige Schwarzer hier?* In other words, what it felt like being the only Black person in the audience? Of course, I was imagined to be out of place. I got it.

How do I forget the hurt I feel when scholarly comrades in the trenches of struggle against epistemic violence, cognitive injustice, and so on, rather embarrassingly pander and defer to Whiteness, or become dispirited when their expectations of the cerebrum of the dark chocolate skin are exceeded? How do I forget the experience of a colleague in Nigeria who regularly hosted students from several German universities for a Hausa language immersion program? On a group visit to a 'big man' in Maiduguri, the White students were ushered in, while their host (a professor of Hausa phonology, trained at the local university and in SOAS, currently a Vice-Chancellor) was asked by the *mai gadi* or the gate man to wait outside. Of course, the Black professor colleague had to be the driver or escort of some sort.

How do I forget how a Ghanaian friend based in Ontario called me at my base in Montreal to go check out an apartment she had been told was available for rent by her brother? The brother was to study in the city. On arriving at the building, my dark chocolate skin gave away what my friend's accent had concealed, and the apartment was gone! If only my friend had confessed over the phone to the crime of being born Black, to parody Trevor Noah's book *Born a Crime*, I may not have wasted the journey! If only we had remembered Wole Soyinka's 1963 poem, 'Telephone Conversation'! (https://www.k-state.edu/english/westmank/spring_00/SOYINKA.html).

For me, then, Sinfree's Virtual Forum series is a 'collaboratory' for connecting the dots and fostering much-needed Pan-Southern discourses that transcend rejoinders.

## Summary of the Chapters

Decolonization of academia was the central theme of our conversation with Kwesi Kwaa Prah in Chapter 1. Exploring some of the arguments put forth in *The Challenge of Decolonizing Education* (Prah, 2018), participants discussed topics concerning multilingual pedagogical strategies in higher education and the role of Indigenous African languages in localized decolonizing efforts. Unpacking central themes in *Linguistics and the Third Reich* (Hutton, 1999), the conversation with Christopher Hutton in Chapter 2 covered the role of linguistics in Nazi Germany, the nature of the relationship between linguistics and race, and the ways in which the politics of mother tongue and language rights might, in some contexts, be treated as liberatory, whilst in others it might be used in an oppressive manner. Discussions with Monica Heller and Bonnie McElhinny, in Chapter 3, revolved around themes presented in *Language, Capitalism, Colonialism* (Heller & McElhinny, 2017). Some of the issues raised in this session included differing views on the notion of hope, imagining what a sociolinguistics from outside the West would look like, and the erasure of Black women scholars in sociolinguistics. The conversation with Robbie Shilliam, presented in Chapter 4, was motivated by his publications 'Behind the Rhodes statue' (Shilliam, 2019) and *The Black Pacific* (Shilliam, 2015). The Rhodes Must Fall Oxford campaign served as a political backdrop to analyze the presence of Black bodies in the Empire's White spaces. Furthermore, we explored distinctions between decolonization and diversity and inclusion initiatives. For example, student engagement in protests was considered to be an iteration of decolonizing praxis with potential to transform the power relations within institutions. Finally, in Chapter 5, the conversation with John Baugh focused on the intersections between language, race and social justice (Baugh, 2020). In particular, participants reflected upon the extent to which (forensic) linguistics may serve to counter practices of race-based linguistic profiling and shed light on the material consequences (e.g. inequitable access to housing) of the discursive (re)production of structures of inequality.

## Conclusion

The original purpose of this Forum has always been to hear voices *above* the prescribed academic disciplines which, in their own way, crack the colonial structure of the intellectual enterprise. Above all, we do not wish to leave those voices only in the academic realm of decolonial projects; decoloniality cannot be limited to a group of eager scholars who meet with a certain frequency via video conferencing. Thus, a hope of this Forum is to go beyond the forum itself, to discuss language shaping and being shaped by relations of race, gender, sexuality in spaces of praxis that instill other ways of understanding, loving, knowing and learning. Those spaces of praxis are contextualized in our institutions, our courts, our community centers, our neighborhoods, our schools, our hometowns.

Each chapter will resonate differently with each reader based on their praxis and their conceptualization of liberation and decoloniality. We hope the chapters included in this first volume on Decolonial Voices encourages readers to work collectively to make cracks in the colonial matrix of power (Mignolo & Walsh, 2018), to see the colonial symbols fall, whether they be Confederate statues, university fees, Covid vaccine lines, or hearing the color of the language.

## References

Anzaldúa, G. (1987) *Borderlands/La Frontera: The New Mestiza*. San Francisco: Aunt Lute Books.

Baugh, J. (2018) *Linguistics in Pursuit of Justice*. Cambridge: Cambridge University Press.

Bhambra, G., Gebrial, D. and Nişancıoğlu, K. (2018) *Decolonising the University*. London: Pluto Press.

Bhambra, G.K. and Holmwood, J. (2021) *Colonialism and Modern Social Theory*. Cambridge: Polity Press.

Chandra, G. and Erlingsdottir, I. (eds) (2021) *The Routledge Handbook of the Politics of the #MeToo Movement*. London: Routledge.

Comaroff, J. (2022) Introduction. In S. Makoni, A. Kaiper-Marquez and L. Mokwena (eds) *Handbook Language in the Global Souths* (pp. forthcoming). London and New York: Routledge.

Comaroff, J. and Comaroff, J. (2011) *Theory from the South: Or, How Euro-America is Evolving towards Africa*. London: Routledge.

Cusicanqui, S. (2019) Ch'ixinakax utxiwa: A reflection on the practices and discourses of decolonization. *Language, Culture, and Society* 1 (1), 106–119. Reprint. https://doi.org/10.1075/lcs.00006.riv

Descola, P. (2013) *Beyond Nature and Culture*. Chicago: University of Chicago Press.

Diagne, S.B. (2021) uBuntu, Nite, and the struggle for global justice. In *African Studies Global Virtual Forum 2021–22: Decoloniality and Southern Epistemologies*. https://www.youtube.com/channel/UC-dIZgdBHmO2zl4FDwVuRmw/videos

Ekotto, F. (2021) Reading Negritude thinkers with Black Lives Matter. In *African Studies Global Virtual Forum 2021–22: Decoloniality and Southern Epistemologies*. https://www.youtube.com/channel/UC-dIZgdBHmO2zl4FDwVuRmw/videos

Fanon, F. (1986) *Black Skin, White Masks*. London: Pluto Press.

Gordon, J. (2022) Interview. In S. Makoni, A. Kaiper-Marquez and L. Mokwena (eds) *Handbook Language in the Global Souths* (pp. forthcoming). London and New York: Routledge.

Heller, M. and McElhinny, B. (2017) *Language, Capitalism, Colonialism: Toward a Critical History*. Toronto: University of Toronto Press.

Horton, M. and Freire, P. (1990) *We Make the Road by Walking: Conversations on Education and Social Change*. Philadelphia, PA: Temple University Press.

Hutton, C. (1999) *Linguistics and the Third Reich: Mother-tongue Fascism, Race and the Science of Language*. London: Routledge.

Ingold, T. (2015) *The Life of Lines*. London and New York: Routledge.

Karkov, N. (2015) Decolonizing praxis in Eastern Europe: Toward a South-to-South dialogue. *Comparative and Continental Philosophy* 7 (2), 180–200.

Kohn, E. (2013) *How Forests Think: Toward an Anthropology beyond the Human*. Berkeley: University of California Press.

Lomeu Gomes, R. (2021) Family multilingualism from a southern perspective: Language ideologies and practices of Brazilian parents in Norway. *Multilingua* 40 (5), 707–734. https://doi.org/10.1515/multi-2019-0080

Makoni, B. (2021) Black female scholarship matters: A black female's reflections on language and sexuality studies. *Journal of Sexuality Studies* 10 (1), 48–58.

Maldonado-Torres, N., Vizcaino, R., Wallace, J. and We, J.E.A. (2018) Decolonizing philosophy. In B. Bhambra, D. Gebrial and K. Nişancıoğlu (eds) *Decolonizing the University* (pp. 64–90). London: Pluto Press.

Mamdani, M. (2020) *Neither Settler nor Native: The Making and Unmaking of Permanent Minorities*. Cambridge, MA: Harvard University Press.

Mignolo, W.D. and Walsh, C.E. (2018) *On Decoloniality: Concepts, Analytics, Praxis*. Durham, NC: Duke University Press.

Mogstad, H. and Tse, L. (2018) Decolonizing anthropology: Reflections from Cambridge. *The Cambridge Journal of Anthropology* 36 (2), 53–72.

Prah, K. (2018) *The Challenge of Decolonizing Education*. Cape Town: Centre for Advanced Studies of African Society.

Pratt, M.L. (1991) Arts of the contact zone. *Profession*, 33–40.

Shilliam, R. (2015) *The Black Pacific: Anti-colonial Struggles and Oceanic Connections*. London: Bloomsbury.

Shilliam, R. (2019) Behind the Rhodes statue: Black competency and the imperial academy. *History of the Human Sciences* 32 (5), 3–27.

Shor, I. (2017) Making Freire's first 'talking book': A Pedagogy for Liberation, 1983–1986. *Rizoma Freireano* 22, 4–5.

Shor, I. and Freire, P. (1987) *A Pedagogy for Liberation: Dialogues on Transforming Education*. South Hadly, MA: Bergin & Garvey.

de Sousa Santos, B. (2016) *Epistemologies of the South: Justice against Epistemicide*. London and New York: Routledge.

de Souza, L.M.T.M. (2022) Towards a decolonization of the silent history of the sociolinguistics of Brazilian Portuguese. In B. Antia and S. Makoni (eds) *Southernizing Sociolinguistics* (pp. forthcoming). London and New York: Routledge.

Soyinka, W. (1963) Telephone conversation. https://allpoetry.com/poem/10379451-Telephone-Conversation-by-Wole-Soyinka

Suárez-Krabbe, J. (2021) Over our dead bodies: The death project, egoism and the existential dimensions of decolonization. In J.F. Carralees and J. Suárez-Krabbe (eds) *Transdisciplinary Thinking from the Global South: Whose Problems, Whose Solutions?* (pp. 130–147). London: Routledge.

Taiwo, O. (2019) Rethinking the decolonization trope in philosophy. *The Southern Journal of Philosophy* 57 (Spindel Suppl.), 135–159. https://doi.org/10.1111/sjp.12344

Tuck, E. and Yang, K.W. (2012) Decolonization is not a metaphor. *Decolonization: Indigeneity, Education & Society* 1 (1), 1–40.

# 1 Language and Decolonization in Institutions of Higher Learning in Africa

Kwesi Kwaa Prah

Kwesi Kwaa Prah is Professor Emeritus of Sociology at the University of the Western Cape. He was Professor Extraordinary at the University of South Africa and is the founder of the Africa-wide Centre for Advanced Studies of African Society. He has worked extensively across Africa, Europe and Asia, researching and teaching sociology and anthropology in various universities and research institutions. In his book, *The Challenge of Decolonizing Education* (Centre for Advanced Studies of African Society, 2018), Dr Prah discusses terms such as decolonizing knowledge and education, nativization, domestication, de-westernization and Indigenization, which all imply 'bringing home', rehabilitating, and making knowledge part of your own belongings – belongings you feel comfortable with, understand, and that have direct cultural bearings.

## Sinfree Makoni

What I'm going to do now is to engage in a conversation with Prof. Prah. I will raise questions from his book, *The Challenge of Decolonizing Education*. What do you mean by decolonizing education? What can African universities learn from South African universities, and what can South African universities learn from African universities?

## Kwesi Kwaa Prah

Universities, or their generic term of reference, tertiary institutions, are a universal type of educational institution. Universities, certainly wherever they may be, have something in common. They are supposed to operate at the apex of knowledge production processes. However, this is done with an eye primarily on resolving and dealing with both scholarly and practical issues as these issues are manifested in their societies. Universities primarily relate to and address issues in the societies in which they are located.

Decolonizing education means stripping the structure and content of the colonially received cultural valuation in education curricula from what is offered, in a purposively emancipating post-colonial context. It requires studious intellectual introspection and the deconstruction of the processes of knowledge production with pin-pointed reflexivity. We must be able to stand outside ourselves and critically objectify ourselves as historical and cultural products. In other words, we must use the basic insights of the sociology of knowledge.

Universities in Africa, south of the north, were introduced during the colonial era. They were to serve the plans and intentions of the colonizers, and this they did. They were cast as close facsimilia of the metropolitan universities of the colonial powers and were meant to train and produce personnel, elites, who would work to ease and facilitate the purposes of the colonialists. This was of course to be expected. The colonialists were not in the business of cultivating social types who would oppose and contradict or undermine their intentions. However, dialectically, it was from the ranks of these elites that modernist resistance to colonialism congealed. Universities in Africa created under colonial aegis were colonial institutions. It stands to reason that with the demise of colonialism the structures, forms and content of these institutions should change to embrace the challenges of greater societal emancipation; that these universities should be regroomed to serve decolonized intent.

What I am saying is that universities have or must have national character. In the first instance, they are focused on questions, as they appear to them, in their societies of residence. They have the character of the society in which they are historically grounded and reflect the cultural characteristics of the societies in which they are located. It therefore means that an African university should necessarily be mainly preoccupied with issues of African society. They cannot be fashioned, structured and directed to the same issues as the university of Oxford, Harvard, Moscow or Beijing. I think that in all these different localities universities develop as historical institutions which are to a large extent culturally formed and determined by the historical, social and cultural features of the societies in which they are based. When that has been said, it is also important to point out that, universities, wherever they may be, also carry universal ideas. Ideas that are cross-culturally recognized and which are therefore largely independent of locality, culture and history. In as far as this universalism is concerned, you can, for example, not say there is a type of mathematics which is African mathematics or Russian chemistry or Chinese mathematics. It is however possible to recognize traditions or particular histories in knowledge gathering, knowledge production, and the recognition of significant antecedents in these processes. But a species of mathematics, chemistry or physics with its own localized logic which is ultimately non-universal does not exist. Thus, it is possible for two or more mathematicians who do not speak each other's languages to silently follow the same logic on a blackboard.

## Makoni

So, you are saying that the starting point for universities should be to address the local and specific problems that they encounter within their immediate environment. They also must adopt the character of their societies. They must adopt the imprint of the societies that they, they're working in. But having said that, you are also saying that universities are universal because they have to enter into dialogue with other universities. So, you equivocate between the impact of the local and the power of the universal in shaping universities.

## Prah

That is not what I am saying. Universities do not, or rather, should not, 'adopt' the imprint of the societies they are working in. The notion of 'adoption' in this sense is vaguely tautological. It is epistemologically redundant. This should happen as a matter of course. This should happen almost automatically if they are true to their meaning of answering questions and needs as they appear in their societies. The point I am making is that we want 'African universities not universities in Africa'. African universities would serve African needs, they are not immediately or competently suited to answer to social and cultural problems located in the Russian or Indian or Chinese experience. The fact that they have universal characteristics they share with other universities across the globe does not mean that they have immediate capacities to deal with any problem anywhere. Of course, they should be in constant dialogue with other universities. This is to be expected. This is needed and indeed this is what happens, but the immediate problems they solve and the issues they face should be issues they are best placed to answer and resolve. There is a dialectical relationship between the local and the universal. Local knowledge assumes universal status if its methodologies and solutions adequately serve the purposes for which they are offered and have cross-cultural relevance. In music, they call this 'variations on a theme'. An additional point that can be made is that we must be national before we become international. We grow from inside outwards. In Hegelian language, thesis precedes antithesis not the other way round.

I need also to point out that, for example, if you look at the historiography of the Second World War, you will find that Russians with, in my view, great reason, say that they largely won the war against Germany. The back of Hitler's 6th Army was broken in Stalingrad in December 1942.

Many British historians claim that Britain won the war. Americans also contend that they won the war. In each of these instances, it would be suggested that the decisive input in winning the war was made by them. For the Chinese, the war started in 1937 with Japan. For the British it started with Germany in 1939. For the US it commenced at Pearl Harbor in 1941 with the Japanese. This is how reality appears to various actors from where they stand. They are looking at the world from their localities, their viewpoints, their histories and their interests. The Chinese describe the 19th century as the 'Century of Shame', starting from the Opium Wars in the late 1830s to the Boxer Rebellion at the end of the century. China took humiliation at the hands of Western imperial powers. Western historians do not describe the 19th century as the century of shame; for them it is the 'triumph of the West'. British historians describe the war [in South Africa] between Boer and Brit as the Boer War. The Boers describe it as the Anglo-Boer war. What I am saying is that people interpret the same event from the vantage point of their own histories.

**Makoni**

The role of the postcolonial elite runs through your work. If universities in South America, Africa or Asia are to become relevant to their local context, the enterprise has to be driven to some extent by local elites. But that means local elites are willing to hand over power, make another dispensation.

**Prah**

That's a very important problem you raise. The issue of the elites. Of course, the enterprise has to be driven by local elites; that means that they must not hand over responsibility, power or initiative to external powers and influences who have their own interests. If they are competent elites who are instrumentally focused on the local conditions and are advised by the local conditionalities, in other words, if they are fully relevant to their local context, the problem is easy to solve. What we see is however different. Our local elites are inordinately beholden to the elites of our former colonial masters. They are neocolonial creatures. They have been formed and shaped in the image of our former masters. They are not free agents. Their thinking is conditioned by the epistemological legacies of the colonial order. Most of our elites take this heritage of compradoral thinking as the natural order of things. They are unable to transcend the epistemological hand-me-downs that the post-colonial order or, better still, the neocolonial order offers us. If our universities and other tertiary institutions are to shed the vestiges of neocolonialism, we need to take a critical stance from what we have inherited and recognize how in a host of instances, the neocolonial heritage alienates us from our own historical, cultural and social realities of existence. Unfortunately, African neocolonial elites believe in the sanctity and supremacy of knowledge encoded in English, French or Portuguese. Latin America is another story. Across the Atlantic, in a not too dissimilar fashion, much of the information transacted in and out of education has been settler-colonial driven.

Therefore, in sum, the answers the elites have for the rest of our societies are not really meaningful for the broader masses of the society. The elites feel more comfortable and happier in the metropolitan centers of the world. The fact is that much of our work is done in colonial languages, which are not properly understood by over 80% of the population. Asian contemporary societies have reached levels of unrivaled development because, to a large extent, they use their own languages in education and in the rest of their social lives.

**Makoni**

You are arguing that the development and the decolonization of Africa cannot succeed without confronting the language question.

**Prah**

Yes, without our own languages, there is no hope at all. I am totally convinced about this. The earlier we start dealing with this issue the better for us. You may want to also note that it is precisely the African elites, the neocolonial elites, who stand firmly in the way and are not allowing us to use our languages fully as languages of education and development at all levels. It is precisely the elites who are addicted to the languages of our former masters, who would want to compete with Shakespeare in his own language, compete with Racine in French and Pessoa in Portuguese. I have always argued that without use of our languages there is no hope for African emancipation and development. The longer we wait the more precarious and painful the journey forward becomes.

## Makoni

Now, with that in mind, I want to go back to the conversation that we had before the formal start of the session about issues of race and ethnicity. You wrote a book called *Beyond the Colour Line*, which was first published in 1998 by Africa World Press (New Jersey/Asmara).

## Prah

Yes. *Beyond the Colour Line* was published when I was at the University of the Western Cape. It is a collection of selected sketches, letters, papers and reviews dealing with issues of Pan Africanism. Some important points I make in the book (pages 36–37) include the fact that:

> The racial definition of an African is flawed. It is unscientific and hence untenable. No serious mind today would use the race concept in any way except as an instrument for poetic imagery. What I am saying is that no group of people has been 'pure' from time immemorial. Notions of purity belong to the language of fascists and the rubbish-bin of science. But before my observations are misunderstood, let me take the argument into another direction. Most Africans are black, but not all Africans are black and not all blacks have African cultural and historical roots. Jews range from blond to black. Another example, Arabs also do. I am not denying the fact that this continent is the cradle of the African and as far as we know today, the birthplace of homo sapiens. There are many groups in Africa today which are not African, do not describe themselves as African or wish to be so regarded, peoples whose culture and histories are linked to and derived from extra-African sources. Needless to say, they are full citizens and must always remain full and equal citizens in all respects to the Africans amongst whom they live, and I dare say apartheid and caste systems of any kind should not be tolerated, since we seek ultimately the freedom of all humanity, and the untrammeled social intercourse of all the peoples of this earth. The cultures of these minorities who live amongst us have helped in the enrichment and cosmopolitanization of social life and tastes in large areas of Africa. Some of these groups may in due course of time and history come to regard themselves as African. All peoples have a right to their culture and its usage. But cultures are not stagnant or fixed entities. Cultural change is a permanent feature of all societies. No human group has from time immemorial been hermetically sealed, culturally or otherwise. Diffusion, interpenetration and mixing is the real substance of the historical process, but at every given historical conjuncture, people are formed by the existent culture they produce and reproduce. But cultures are created

and also wither. When cultures die, the people whose culture declines and falls do not necessarily physically die, they become other people. Often they are absorbed by more dominant cultures.

I wrote this over 30 years ago and my views on these matters remain the same.

In Africa, south of the Sahara, you would find that, in each country you go into, 95% or more of the people, except in the settler-colonial states, are indigenes, but there are also minorities. This sort of mix is not different from the rest of the world. If you go to Britain, 90% of the people may be originally from the British Isles but today Britishers come from all corners of the globe.

## Makoni

What about Scotland?

## Prah

Yes. Scotland became part of the United Kingdom early in the 18th century. Scotland has, like many other parts of the world, also absorbed people from other areas, particularly the English and the Irish. But they have also contributed to the making of other peoples in all parts of the world, especially as Presbyterians to Northern Ireland. We have minorities on the African continent from other parts of the world. It's just about in the same proportions of minorities that there are in other parts of the world. But the important difference is that the minority European and Arab cultures in Africa are wherever they are the ruling cultural groups, reference groups. They are the prosperous cultures that dominate and guide the social process in these societies. I don't think, in most of Africa, for example, when you go to an African village in West Africa, you can legitimately with reason bother people with questions about color; the normative color is Black. It is in Europe and particularly America that there is fixation and undisguised discrimination on the basis of color. There is incessant chatter about color and obsessions with color all the time. This is understandable because Blacks in America are relentlessly discriminated against. 'Black Lives Matter' is no small matter! The United States claims to be the leading democratic society in our world. But it is also, at the same time, unable to completely forsake voter suppression and is one of the most racist countries in the world. In that sense American capitalist democracy is in practice deeply flawed. It is systemically racist.

## Makoni

But what about the situation in the Sudan?

## Prah

From the middle of the 7th century AD Arabization processes in the Sudan have been ongoing. Until well into the 20th century Arab-led slavery of Africans was quietly countenanced. You can't tell identity differences between people on the basis of color in the Sudan. Most of those who claim to be Arabs in the Sudan are Black. The identity differences in the Sudan are not really physical, they are cultural and religious. For human beings everywhere in the world, what is important and needed is the legitimate recognition of cultural differences and tolerance, the acceptance of the rights of people as cultural groups. Color intrinsically is not really relevant. The main issue is cultural tolerance and the need to be able to have open cultural spaces. By cultural space, I do not mean physical space, I mean the freedom to practice, live and celebrate our cultures in the collective understanding that cultural diversity enriches us all.

## Magda Madany-Saá

I do my research in Latin America, so I wanted to ask you, as in your 2018 book *The Challenge of Decolonizing Education* published by CASAS, and now also, you pinpointed how important language is for decolonizing education. I wanted to ask you what models of decolonized education you have in mind in the context where the language of the colonizer is not only the official language of the country but actually is the language that is spoken. In Latin American contexts, what would be a viable model for decolonizing education in such a country?

## Prah

That's a brilliant question. I think we should be guided by the wider and deeper principles of democracy and tolerance. We live in a world that is becoming increasingly small, with people living culturally on top of each other. The only way we can survive as a human community is to have wisdom and the sense and democratic instinct to tolerate cultural differences without creating any barriers for people crossing cultural lines.

In South America settler-colonists have reduced the numbers of Native Americans to minorities. These minorities do not have the cultural space or the possibility to develop their languages, so you have situations of internal colonialism. Except for the Andean states, the indigenes have been reduced everywhere to small minorities. Their languages and cultures have been degraded to inferior status. They need to be allowed to develop their languages and cultures to equality in these societies.

This applies also to the United States, with respect to the Native Americans; people who have lived there for thousands of years. The real owners of the land. The US 'melting pot' idea is in reality intolerant of cultural diversity. Native Americans have been pushed into reservations, their languages trampled upon, with no possibility of modernizing these languages. If we want a world in which we all can exist in freedom, then this must change. The same thing is true for the Sami people in places like Norway, Russia, Sweden and Finland. The languages of people in Sápmi are trampled upon in some of the most democratic societies of the world. And so, the problem is a large one, as we move forward.

We should provide resources for the Aboriginal peoples of Latin America to develop their languages, as languages of science and technology, and so multilingual language policies are crucial for social development. Multilingualism is the solution for a culturally and demographically incommodious world. When I went to study in the Netherlands, in the beginning of the 1960s, I was surprised to find that the lectures were in Dutch, of course, but the recommended books would be, you know, in English, French, German or Dutch. It was assumed that students entering university would have working knowledge of these languages because in the previous levels of education they are given sufficient educational exposure to these languages.

In Africa most of what we call languages are in fact variants of 'core language' clusters which can share the same spelling system. If you teach these languages properly, if you write them with unified orthographies, then it should be possible to have institutions where you can recommend textbooks that are written in one variety or other but can be used by speakers who use a different variety. For example, slightly different varieties of KiSwahili are spoken in Uganda, Kenya, Tanzania, Malawi, North Mozambique and the Congo. Contemporary Africa especially urban Africa has become a veritable hot bed of multilingualism, African language multilingualism. The overwhelming majority of urban Africans today are comfortably multilingual. It is a blessing.

But this is mainly oral multilingualism. It needs to become literate multilingualism.

### Madany-Saá

Thank you very much, Dr Prah, for this answer. We have plenty more questions. So, I will now switch to Susan. Thank you so much for writing your question. So, if you wish, you can personally ask your question to Prof. Prah.

### Susan Coetzee-Van Rooy (North-West University, South Africa)

Professor, you've basically answered my question. When you started to refer to multilingualism, I marveled at the multilingualism of African people, and we never do something in one language only; we always use sets of languages to perform functions.

At North-West University, we are implementing multilingualism. But we are saying that children and students are welcome to bring all of the languages they have in their minds, and we will develop multilingual pedagogy. And I think the multilingual policy was successfully implemented at the University of Cape Town by Madiba. I'm sure he's carrying it out at Stellenbosch now. I think we are all becoming multilingual. I'm not really sure that fighting for one language early in education, no matter where it is, is a good principle.

### Prah

I can hear from the way you speak English that you are originally Afrikaans. Afrikaans is one of the linguistic miracles of the last 150 years. Languages which have moved from zero or close to zero to languages of development in no time. The other examples of languages in the world, which have made that big jump to modernity, are Modern Hebrew in Israel and Bahasa in Indonesia and Malaysia. There is a very interesting point about Afrikaans. Since the 19th century, from the 1820s till the end of the century, most of the conflict between the Boers and the English on the cultural level was about language. We go on in circles. I have lived in South Africa for a quarter of a century now. We're still talking endlessly about language policies in Africa with little or no real progress in multilingual policy formulation and implementation.

## Madany-Saá

Thank you. So let's move on. We have interesting questions about the distinction between languages as spoken and as institutionalized.

## Bert van Pinxteren (Leiden University, The Netherlands)

There seems to be a tendency, when we're talking about African languages, to say, 'Oh, there are so many of them, and all of them are welcome, and all functional, and should be treated the same way'. For scientific discourse, I think we should not lose sight of the need to develop standardized varieties. In African languages, if we continue to be blindfolded by the trope that there are 2,000 African languages and, 'Oh, it's so complicated to develop them all', then we're going to render ourselves powerless, and we're going to hand over to the dominance of English. That's the sort of self-castration that goes on in the circles of African linguists.

## Prah

In fact, there are not so many languages as people make them out to be, but there are often different labels for the same language. The languages themselves are not so many. I mean, take Pulaar as an example. It has the biggest linguistic-geographical spread in Africa. It is one language which in slightly differing varieties is spoken in 17 countries.

African languages are not many if you put them into clusters. If you put them into clusters that are structurally and lexically similar, then they are sufficiently similar for us to be able to write them with the same rules of spelling.

## Lynn Mario de Souza (University of São Paulo, Brazil)

I am familiar with only a couple of your articles. Well, I'd like to go back to the initial discussion of the local and the universal, when you talked about the colonizing of the university, because what I see is that knowledge is like languages – occurring in ecologies – when what actually separates knowledge and makes knowledge into universal or local is a relationship of power. So, what we consider to be universal knowledge or a universal language is little more than a language or a set of knowledges that is wielded by groups of power. So, for the question about local knowledge as being different from universal knowledge – the universal is simply someone's local, but not just anyone's; the language of that group that is more powerful in a particular ecology becomes the national language, which, I think, is what has happened with Hindi in India, with Bahasa in Indonesia, with Portuguese in Brazil. You're talking about Afrikaans and modern Hebrew as being modern languages. I would say Brazilian Portuguese is also one of these when it is Portuguese in Brazil. Or we could say that occurs when we produce knowledge in our local language. But, on the other hand, exactly what we call our local language in Brazil is not the local language of our Indigenous communities.

On a world scale, we are totally excluded from knowledge production, unless we do it in English. So, what I'm saying is that I'm trying to maintain this level of complexity when we're dealing with a university, it believes it has either local or universal or languages, and these are seen as either national or not. I'm trying to go beyond that. In your last comments, you referred to this idea of saying that we're always multilingual, and this conception of being multilingual is complex, especially in contexts like Africa, where there are many languages that co-exist because it comes down to our concept of language as objectified and bordered or not. These languages that co-exist may be given different names but they may also be, for some, the 'same' language. So, what is the 'same' language and what are different languages can vary immensely. Take the situation, for example, of the Scandinavian languages.

I would like to come back to this notion of decolonization. The whole discussion of decolonization needs to recuperate this level of complexity, rather than having to go back to pre-colonial notions of language, where we fall back into discussions of homogeneity. Whose homogeneity? Ours or theirs? You know, I would appreciate your thinking on this.

## Prah

Well, thank you. Brazilian Portuguese is too close to metropolitan Portuguese to be regarded as a separate language. Please remember also that the aboriginal peoples of Brazil are being systematically deculturized. They are facing ethnocide. In Japan, the Ainu language has almost died out. The Uighurs in China are teetering on the brink. In Francoist Spain, from the mid-1930s onwards, languages other than Spanish/Castilian were banned from official discourse. It is only since the 1970s that the linguistic ecology has become more open and tolerant. It is possible to restore and develop a dying pre-colonial language. The Irish have tenuously been able to do it. I think one useful thing about your argument is that you say you want to separate the universality of knowledge from questions of the universal pretensions of language. I don't think that language equals knowledge. That is wrong. Language is an instrument for processing, packaging and transmitting knowledge. But language is also a record of the history of the people, the users of the language. It is the register of the experience of people, the users of the language. People prosper as their language develops.

## de Souza

But is 'knowledge' not conveyed in some languages and not others?

## Prah

No single or chosen languages convey knowledge. All languages can convey knowledge if they are empowered and enabled to do so. Language carries knowledge. It is the instrument that carries and transacts knowledge, but knowledge is not language. Different languages can carry the same knowledge. One is an instrument for the handling of the other. I'm talking about the local and the universal, independent of language. I'm talking about knowledge. Knowledge that is universal tends to be localized by different communities into their own languages. The development of language is the development of people, the people who speak that language.

The advancement, the possibility of advancement of the overwhelming majority of the people in any society will be limited if the languages of the majorities are not utilized. Literacy is a key issue. We have hardly talked so far about literacy. The key issue in the whole discussion, in a sense, is about literacy in contrast with orality. Literacy enhances language movement; I mean linguistic mobility both geographically and historically, in space and time. Literacy underwrites cultural permanence. It impinges directly on the question of the local and universal. Without literacy, knowledge development cannot be scaled up and carried across space and time.

The creative genius of humanity is embedded in language, your language. Can you compete with an Englishman in his language? Have you ever seen a society that is effectively developing through somebody else's language? No society on Earth makes serious mass-based progress using someone else's language. You see, what will happen if we follow the suggestion you're making regarding acquiescence to the minority languages of power and dominance is that the larger majorities in the world in Africa and Asia will forever be culturally dominated. The culturally endangered minorities in the Americas, Africa, Asia and Europe will be pushed over the edge. I don't know whether we have a right to say to the people of Africa or anywhere else, please accept the fact of becoming an Englishman and become an Englishman. Lose your African character, lose your culture, lose your language, and become English or French or Arab. I don't think that is right. And I don't think it's justified. It's an argument you can make. But I'm not so sure whether it has very much democratic currency for the people on the African continent or anywhere else. Every country in which the language of a minority is being utilized as the official language, it is a language of power and dominance. In such circumstances, you have a colonial, neocolonial or internal colonial situation.

## Makoni

I'm grateful that you can find time to discuss your ideas about language with us.

## References

Prah, K.K. (1998) *Beyond the Colour Line: Pan-Africanist Disputations: Selected Sketches, Letters, Papers and Reviews*. New Jersey/Asmara: Africa World Press.

Prah, K.K. (2018) *The Challenge of Decolonizing Education*. Cape Town: Centre for Advanced Studies of African Society.

# 2 Linguistics, Race and Fascism

Christopher Hutton

## Sinfree Makoni

Welcome all of you again to this session and I'd like to express my deep gratitude to Chris Hutton for finding the time first of all to write the book that will be the main focus of our discussion and then too for his willingness to take part in this discussion.

Chris Hutton's research focus is on political issues in language and linguistics. At present he is investigating the links between linguistic theory and race theory, following on from his 1999 book of linguistics and ideology in Nazi Germany (*Linguistics and the Third Reich*) which we are going to be discussing. In addition to his interest in the history and politics of Western linguistics, Chris is pursuing various projects at the intersection of linguistics, law and intellectual history. The focus in this work is on issues of legal definition and classification. His publications include *Race and the Third Reich* (2005), *Definition in Theory and Practice* (2007, with Roy Harris) and *Language, Meaning and the Law* (2009). More recently he has published two books *Integrationism and the Self: Reflections on the Legal Personhood of Animals* and *The Tyranny of Ordinary Meaning: Corbett v Corbett and the Invention of Legal Sex* (both 2019). Under preparation is a book-length study on the concept of Aryan.

Chris, I'd like to engage in an informal discussion with you concerning this book. But let me situate my question in a bigger context so that you understand where I am coming from. Last month we discussed *Language, Colonialism, Capitalism* by Monica Heller and Bonnie McElhinny (see Chapter 3). What is interesting about it was that they were trying to provide an account of the historical evolution of socio-linguistics, language studies and African studies in Canada and North America. But your context is different, it is Nazi Germany. So, in a sense, the two books are linked in that in both cases, we are looking at the development of linguistics or ideas about language in very specific localities, during very specific historical periods. That is the general idea.

I and a colleague of mine at the University of the Western Cape, Bellville, South Africa, Bassey Antia, following your work and that of Heller and McElhinny, are interested in trying to work out the history of ideas about language in different regions of the world particularly in the Global South. We therefore are drawing quite extensively on your work. So that is where I stand.

Now let me continue and ask very specific, albeit pedantic questions. In the acknowledgements to your book, you say for example that you learned many lessons in thinking laterally about linguistics from Roy Harris. What does it mean to think laterally in linguistics?

## Christopher Hutton

I guess Harris had a way of picking up an idea, decontextualising it, and analysing it. When I was a student, I found it very refreshing because he didn't take anything for granted and he was a kind of intellectual historian himself. So, he had a way, I think, of placing discussions of linguistics in a wider historical, social context and that really caught my imagination, actually. And I think also, he just never believed anything anybody said, actually [laughter]. So, he was just, you know, he was a contrarian.

I must say when I started reading the linguistics of Nazi Germany, I was quite surprised, shocked because it's actually quite normal, in some sense. So, that was challenging. So, I guess, also the idea of not to take as given the notion of a language, which is also important in your thinking about language and linguistics. This is another way of looking at this notion of language, *a* language, in a very specific political, social context. And seeing actually the different kinds of effects this ideology can have or how it works itself out and the role the linguists play as ideologues.

Because North America is the default place and, you know, I grew up in the sort of Chomskyan era where there was no direct connection between formal linguistics and social reality. I mean, there's obviously links that you can draw, but you have to find them. So, I think, by looking at Nazi Germany, you can find these, you can see this much more clearly there and then think back about other contexts.

## Makoni

Okay, right. Let me take you back a bit, because we are scattered across the globe. I have some idea about who Roy Harris is, but I think my other colleagues in the audience might not have. Can you just provide us with some background on who Roy Harris is and what you think has been his major contribution to linguistic scholarship?

## Hutton

He was Professor of General Linguistics at Oxford and he was, in a way, a very English establishment figure, but he was also a contrarian, as I said. And he led a kind of mini revolt within the British academic establishment, basically, attacking what he saw as a central set of beliefs that linguistics fostered in the Western tradition. He normally talked about the 'Western tradition'. So, there's an interesting debate one could have there. Specifically, the notion of languages as autonomous entities, he called it the *language myth* and also the idea that words were determinate in form and meaning and, therefore, there could be a class of experts called linguists whose job it was, as it were, to analyse and to make authoritative statements about this object of study. So, what interested me, partly, was this notion of authority, and I think that's very relevant to Southern Theory in the sense that who has the authority in a particular society to pronounce upon and be an expert about language?

That's something I've thought about more in recent years, but it was definitely implicit in his thinking. He was extremely unpopular in British linguistics... anyway, that's a long story, but he was basically shut out. He kept publishing. He wrote, maybe too much, actually. He also wrote influentially on the subject of literacy and writing, which is another central issue, I guess if you're thinking globally about literacy and writing. Again, he didn't take for granted a definition of writing, for instance. So, that's interesting and challenging. So, even people who hate his general linguistics often find his work on writing very interesting and provocative. He was a bit before his time in a way, because it's now become a kind of commonplace to attack the construct of a language, though in a different political context... you know this as well as I do.

## Makoni

You know, what is interesting is how some of his ideas are beginning to permeate even to some extent mainstream applied linguistics. For example, the individuals who write about translanguaging now make it a point, once in a while, to make some reference that 'Oh yes, what Harris said about language...' and they proceed and they say what they want even if in some cases it is contrary to what Harris says. Harris is therefore getting into the mainstream of applied linguistic thought. This leads me to my other question. Do you think that Roy Harris's notions of integrational linguistics are compatible with the popular views on translanguaging? Or are these two completely different projects?

## Hutton

They meet at some point but I think the political framework of translanguaging, Harris would probably not have felt comfortable with. Maybe not with some of the identity politics... That's why people read him as conservative I think, because he had a certain rhetorical style, which is very at odds with people who do translanguaging. But I think there is an important genealogy and he is part of that. To try and think outside this construct of a language and what does it mean. You are the one who was asking a few years ago 'What's applied integrationism?'. People who are doing translanguaging are often thinking about actual classroom practice. He didn't go that far.

## Makoni

The other thing that I found interesting in your book, and in some of your writing, is the relationship between linguistics and race theory. You say, for example, that linguistics is both the parent and child of race theory. In a context in which issues about race, White supremacy, xenophobia are increasingly affecting all our lives, can you elaborate a little bit on what you mean by saying that linguistics here is both the parent and child of race theory?

## Hutton

If you look at, say, the beginnings of race theory, it comes partly out of comparative anatomy. And then basically it drew from ideas about *Volk* and nationhood which were really ideas that linguists and others were articulating. So, I see that race theory sort of entered the European intellectual, ideological mainstream marked by ideas which come from a much older tradition about national character, language and territory and so on.

So, there's a kind of struggle in the 19th century between ideas of nationhood, language, territory and the hard race theorists who were looking at physical characteristics. There's an intellectually very confused battle. But anyway, by 'the child' I mean that eventually race theory drops out because it becomes intellectually marginalised after the Second World War. So, in a way, linguistics is still standing as a kind of arbiter of classifying people.

This doesn't directly relate to what's happening in the US. I always think the US is both globally dominant and highly unusual in some ways. I was thinking more of the European context or perhaps the postcolonial context. That's a very sweeping statement. But I do think we should need to read the history of these two disciplines together. And also, see the older lineages, the *Volk*, the idea of 'folk', which is in the Bible actually: language, lineage, territory and culture. And that idea, for good and ill, is there, permeating the Western tradition, and got spread through colonialism and so on. And it runs into this radical, new discipline called race theory or race science – which says actually that what you call a *Volk* is a false unity and you need to read nations through the prism of race. Anyway, it's a very difficult story to get straight. I'm still struggling with it.

## Makoni

This is a very important story to all of us at this point in time, I think, whether in Africa, Europe or the United States, to be able to handle issues about linguistic theory and race theory, more or less, concurrently.

Following that, then, my next question is this. You write that the pursuit of objective scholarly standards does not involve the rejection of prejudice. Now when I was reading this, I was trying to understand what you meant here. You then proceed to say that the pursuit of objective scholarly standards is a commitment to a different type of discourse. In other words, if I am going to be reductionist, are you saying that I can be both the racist and the linguist?

## Hutton

In the terms of that period, yes. In fact, this is a slight problem we have today. If you go through the history of ideas, most people were racists, right. I was thinking, you know, that expertise can formalise a kind of prejudice. People within a particular context can't see something as a prejudice even, it's so much part of their world that they can't step outside to analyse it, but they have a method and they have a sense of being an objective person pursuing a truth and they follow it, sincerely. But, when we look back, we see all these things misshapen by ideology and so on. Because people will look back at us and say similar things. No doubt.

### Makoni

That part is interesting because you say somewhere else that the 'question of the status and objectivity of linguistic methodology is complex' and then you put in parentheses. It's not directly addressed in this book. That's why I'm asking now. You write as follows: 'however there can surely be no reason to argue that linguistics enjoys any special autonomy or privilege in relation to ideology' (Hutton, 1999: 4). Now, let me try this on you… you are then saying that, to some extent, linguistics is not objective and you've just talked about issues of the native speakers, native speaker intuition, natural language processing, etc. Are you then saying that since the notions of natural language processing, native speaker intuition, etc., that, to some extent, belong to psycholinguistics… are you then saying that psycholinguistics is an exercise in language ideology? That it is covertly a language ideological artefact, although they don't say so when they're talking of natural language processing, they're making an ideological statement.

### Hutton

I would have to say, yes. I mean, the problem in linguistics is the moment you enter a field of language and start labelling things you've inevitably fallen into an ideological activity, right. It doesn't mean it's necessarily pernicious, I think that should be said, actually. And then the idea of intuition, which is there in Chomskyan linguistics, actually relates to Romanticism and the notion that an untutored native speaker has these acts of pure intuition and these can be drawn on by the technocratic linguist, you know, and so this is an artefact of a particular ideology. But I think there is a danger in just pointing the finger at people and going 'Ideological! Ideological!' And it's also annoying to people when you do that. I think any labelling activity around language, for example if you have a study and you say 'native speakers of French', you've already entered this complicated field, because you've got to decide if someone comes to you from Martinique or somewhere, so all these problems will arise which are not necessarily apparent if you're sitting in the metropolitan capitals… and I think that's where the, you know, the US and English comes in… because English is like the water that fish swim in, in a way. Which is very different from the cultural politics around language in most of the world, actually. Not that there isn't politics around English in America. Anyway, sorry, that was a rambling answer…

### Makoni

That was really helpful. The part where I spent a lot of time thinking about, reflecting and agonising was the following. You say that 'Nazism was an ideological coalition, and one of the fundamental elements in that coalition was the defence of mother-tongue rights: Nazism was a language-rights movement' (Hutton, 1999: 4). Now this is where this thing gets interesting... I wish I knew this 20 years ago that Nazism was a language rights movement. Of course, I mean, one hopes that not all language rights movement are Nazi. But you're pointing out how discussions about mother-tongue rights and Nazism could co-exist. And given my personal interest in language policy, language planning and language rights, I thought the statement was very sobering indeed. Perhaps you could explain this a little bit more in the context of Nazi Germany.

### Hutton

I think I have in the chapters on Weisgerber and Kloss. So, I've been thinking about it a lot that the language politics of the interwar Europe are such that... radical nationalists in Germany and elsewhere, one of their main concerns is the language rights of Germans who are outside the German state. And this is, on the whole, a right-wing very ultra conservative concern... so language rights become a tool for threatening or intimidating neighboring states and so the fear is that these German speakers will be lost if the Volk assimilates. And there's a similar fear about North America in Germany, but these are not neighboring states. In the context of Europe, there are territorial claims associated with this. And, of course, if you look at Europe, even today, there are all these frozen territorial claims based on language, you know, Hungary, Romania, and so on, based on language or Volk. The case of Kloss explains this, because Kloss is a Nazi in Nazi Germany, but when he comes to North America, there's a whole different context there where it's just about trying to maintain these mother tongues within a different kind of governance framework. So, it's not about fighting for territory. It's about trying to keep people's, you know, immigrant languages alive. So, the framework is totally different. But within the European context, in the interwar context, it was a far-right sort of way of thinking about the map of Europe and so you dream of basically reintegrating your lost speakers into the nation. So that was one of the, you know, one of the strands of radical nationalism that feeds into Nazism.

### Makoni

It's good that you have raised the question about Kloss because that will be the last question that I want to touch on before opening the discussion. You say that the case of Heinz Kloss raises a number of complex questions. Firstly, there are historical questions about the interrelationships and power struggles between various organizations. Then you proceed to say that there is also the question of his own life and work and how he, as an individual scholar, fits into the complex set of institutional, social and intellectual conventions. This leads on to the broader question of Kloss's work. Does it make any difference, in his place within linguistics, if we knew he had a Nazi background? Let me explain why this is interesting or disturbing a bit to me. In language policy and planning – I do a bit of work in that area when I have time – one of the key views is that it's a quest for some form of social justice. Whether you deliberately go out to establish that future that you think you want people to realise... you may not say that in every paper, but generally that is the broader idea. So, when you meet figures, like Kloss, who are Nazi or who have a Nazi background, but who are also engaged in a similar enterprise, it forces you to rethink what is it about language planning and policy or linguistics that makes it so amenable to fascists. What is it about this discipline, I mean, coming from Africa, what is it about linguistics that makes it so historically and viscerally tied to colonialism? Then, in the book that you wrote, what is it about linguistics that makes it amenable to fascism? What is it about linguistics that ties it to White supremacy? That sort of level of self-reflection is a question that is being sort of forced upon some of us by the current world developments. You want to know what is it that makes this discipline, in different historical epochs, amenable to colonialism and Nazism? Given the fact that there is the counter-movement, let's say, of critical scholarship in which you are trying to change the world. But there's still another dimension to it, to applied linguistics, which ties it to all these fascist movements.

## Hutton

If you look at Fishman and Weinreich, I examined two pieces by them. In *Languages in Contact* Weinreich quotes about 20 Nazi linguists. And Fishman, I think, gets from Weinreich this long list of really nasty antisemites... So, there's a bit of a puzzle there in Uriel Weinreich. His father, Max, wrote one of the first books on Nazi scholarship. So, there's a little moment of continuity in American sociolinguistics with Nazi Germany, not in the actual ideas, strictly speaking. I mean, I'm not calling either Fishman or Weinreich, you know, anything like a Nazi. But there is something odd about linguistics. Because it can work for an authoritarian state, it can work for colonialism, it can work for missionaries, it can work for *völkisch* Nazis, it can work for universalist Chomskyans. You know, so there's something very fascinating about this malleability, but also this set of assumptions that seem to run through all these different strands. I think one thing that linguistics can allow you to think about is sort of this perfect integration of people. If you look at even Saussure there's a kind of mind merge where we're all speaking the same language. Therefore there's something powerful conceptually, you know. So, linguistics can be used to imagine forms of social integration. And that of course can be used politically in many different ways. In a postcolonial context, you're striving to renew or to reform, or to integrate. Whereas in Nazi Germany there's also a sense that modernity, or the West or, whoever, universalism, attacking the roots of your culture. It's actually full of paranoia and fear, Nazi Germany. You have France, this is universalism, and you have Anglo-American capitalism, which are kind of Jewish in their mind, you know, and universalist. They feel beleaguered, that's why they assert this culture of difference which linguistics also allows you to do. It gives you a way of mapping a conceptual world. So, Weisgerber can show you 'Oh, we're different. Look at our conceptual patterns. They're different from yours, from the English' and so on. But in my view there should be more writing on Leninist states, or whatever you want to call them. Vietnam, China, Laos. There is some, but I think the anthropologists have done much more in actually looking at how these... because China and Vietnam basically have used linguists and anthropologists to set up these social categories of so-called minorities. So, in China, you have Russian/Soviet linguists in the early 1950s who are basically advising about how to organise the, the nationalities policy. There's not much literature. There's a bit in English, but not... I mean, this is one of the biggest language planning policies in world history. You've got the whole of China, basically. Anyway, I think there is a sort of political history of linguistics to be written. Not by me, I'm too old, but...

## Makoni

Thanks for this wonderful conversation. I will now hand over to Magda to open up the conversation to everybody.

## Magda Madany-Saá

Thank you so much, Dr Makoni. I have already two questions in the chat. I will quickly read them so that Dr Hutton will have time to address them. Question number one. This is a very interesting book which clarified a lot of things for me especially why I felt uncomfortable with psycholinguistic approaches to second language acquisition as I could not identify with the idea of ultimate attainment/ advanced intuitions. After reading this book, I sort of get it. However, looking at it in the current context where there is a reawakening of racial violence, I find myself wondering, if linguistics is both a parent and child of race theory, what does it mean to teach linguistics, as if Black Lives Mattered?

## Hutton

Wow. I'm sort of hampered because I'm sitting in Hong Kong and we have our own issues... for me, one answer, I know it's not a good answer, is to go into the history of things. Because I think when you look at the history, you do see these latent ideologies which when you're looking at something as a practice in a discipline, you miss when these concepts are applied. That's why I found history to be so useful because it reframes things, and you can also trace the institutional history of ideas. And there is the idea that cognitive processes are somehow inside the head. This is something which tends to depoliticise and to decontextualise. I don't have a good answer, honestly. I do find that reading the history of ideas tends to make life more difficult and challenging. And I think some of the most commonplace things that are in front of us are the things that we need history for in order to look at them properly. Back to Harris. I think Harris had a way of taking a commonplace idea and walking around it and standing back from it and giving it a lineage, not always in a political way but... and I think that's something which we can do with ideas in the disciplines that we have. I don't know, Sinfree, if you want to add something.

## Makoni

There are two sets of issues here. Let me focus on the native speaker intuitions then I'll move on to the issue and discussions about Black Lives Matter. I've always wondered, for example, I think people in the audience can help me here. Whether in other languages, for example, whether it's Afrikaans, or whether it's Swahili or Arabic… whether there's an equal preoccupation with discussions about native speaker intuitions or this is one of those bizarre phenomena that are associated with English only? Because I am not sure, for example, when I encounter speakers of African languages, that being a native speaker of an African language matters at all, I'm not sure about that. My other colleagues may correct me on this. What I'm trying to say is that I think what is happening here is that there are certain ways of thinking about English which then get transposed to other languages, and that's my initial view about it. Then the issue about ultimate attainment. I think ultimate attainment raises fundamental problems because the institutions will always find a way of saying you have not met the criteria. It's not you who determines whether you've met the criteria. It's somebody else. So, when second language acquisition is talking about ultimate attainment, I think what they've done, unintentionally, is to buy into the institutional nature of language learning without saying so. Because it is the institutions which determine ultimately whether you've met that particular criterion.

The challenge about the Black Lives Matter thing, what it does, I think, is this. I don't see how courses in applied linguistics, or in linguistics in the US in the Fall and beyond will not include issues about language and race. You could take a course in sociolinguistics in the US and avoid discussions about race, talk about language and ethnicity, language and class. But what the Black Lives Matter people have done is to force us to think about the impact of race and language in terms of the work that we do. That's how I see it. Oh, Raj has a question.

## Kanavillil Rajagopalan (University of Campinas, Brazil)

Prof. Hutton, it's very nice to be talking to you like this. I met you some years ago in Hong Kong during a conference and I still remember that day. I've been thinking of a claim that you've made in several places. The fact that we, as linguists, are some-how still stuck in the 19th-century mentality; that linguistics is basically a 19th-century discipline and we haven't moved from that. My question now is: is it at all possible to come out of that free? Are we still stuck? Are we destined to be stuck in that kind of thinking? Is it at all possible to start with a 'clean slate', as it were, and rethink what language is all about afresh?

## Hutton

It's much easier to criticise that than to propose, but I think that translanguaging is an attempt to get out of this legacy. I also think that Roy Harris tried very hard. We're talking now about the radically contextual nature of language. So, the whole assumptions of the 19th-century scholarship, you know, in a way, fall away because we're left with something which is much more provisional, transitory and constructed micro-socially. I guess it sort of relates to the question before, you know, to what extent are we prisoners of the categories? And I think, again, this has to be looked at institutionally and also by, you know, in terms of different national contexts as well. I do think, you know, Harris was an Oxford professor. You can sit in Oxford and say language is a construct and so on. It's an intellectually very powerful statement. But, let's say you're doing an English language test in China because you want to study in the US. You don't have the luxury of thinking that rules consist of reifications, you know. There is the whole institution of language testing, which is a global money-making machine. And, as Sinfree was saying, in a sense, there's an institutional rationale for that which we all are partly blind to, right? So, I feel I don't have a good answer. I've also thought a lot about lexicography because I've been toying with the idea of doing weird dictionaries, you know. I'm always struck… trying to follow the Hong Kong situation and I look in my Chinese dictionary. I can't find most of the concepts that are being circulated in society. I started making my own list, you know, my own kind of guerrilla dictionary. So that is not theoretically exciting, maybe, but it's actually, I think, lexicography and what it means to document a language is also something which we can think about, it gives a certain amount of scope to think differently. But, in a way, the postwar 20th century was about trying to get out of the 19th century and it's been a very difficult struggle, I think, including the nation-state order, the disciplines and so on. But thank you for your question. I haven't answered it well.

## Madany-Saá

Thank you. I have more questions in the chat box.

As a South African I was obviously struck by the knowledge I had of their [Nazi] assumptions about the special place of the mother tongue and how it also played out in South Africa during the apartheid time. As an African I was also struck by the notion that, in that dispensation, multilingualism was seen as something promiscuous. What I wondered about was what do we know about the place of mother tongue in precolonial Africa? For example, what would the place of the mother tongue be in precolonial Africa before its contact with these European ideas, for example, those expressed in the Third Reich.

There is a little follow-up. I can also not even begin to think about an answer, but I wonder if the World Englishes type of approach is not helpful. For example, remembering that there are many ways of making meaning. And when we teach linguistics to remember to marvel at as many ways to make meaning as possible.

## Hutton

I think Sinfree was hinting at the notion… people you meet as you move through a society, to divide them into native speakers and non-native speakers is a spurious artefact of, maybe, a particular way of looking at language. There is the sense that missionaries and colonial administrators, they didn't try and eradicate vernacular languages, but they did organise them, label them and they put them into social positions. And this concept of mother tongue is, I think, originally a European concept. What colonial linguistics does, it creates a situation or a set of dilemmas which the postcolonial state, in a way, cannot solve. They're almost an insoluble tangle. And this is where Fishman and others were much more optimistic in the beginning that they could somehow think about engineering better solutions. But actually the problems are much deeper and much more difficult. Obviously, I don't know about precolonial Africa but I strongly suspect that you can't find this mother tongue term in precolonial Africa. But, of course, I could be wrong. I'm hesitant to pronounce all this in this company or any company. But there is an idea, which could also be a romantic idea, that precolonial societies live in continua. And, maybe, that's also over-romanticising them because pre-colonial societies had their own language hierarchies. I think there is an important and difficult question because we're trying to look back through this very powerful framework, which is European romanticism plus European universalism, which are both struggling within European linguistics, I think. This is the big battle and it's very difficult to think yourself outside this kind of framework. And also, I think, a precolonial society which is Islamic, say, would have obviously a language hierarchy and a high language, Quranic Arabic and so on. So, they have all kinds of issues about religion and authority and so on. Peter Mühlhäusler and R.A.W. Dixon talk about the Pacific, and I think they saw these Pacific societies as sort of more egalitarian and in continua. And they saw missionaries as creating hierarchies. This is a really key issue for Southern Theory and linguistics, but that's about as far as I could go, I think.

## Makoni

I'm willing to risk my reputation and say the following: in precolonial Africa, you had communication, but it was not through mother tongues. What colonial encounters did, one of the consequences of missionary intervention, was then the creation of those mother tongues. And the mistake made in language policy is that they then seek to try and facilitate communication through these mother tongues that were being created. But, in most cases, most of the interaction is largely through communication. So, the thinking is back to front in the sense that if you adopt an integrationist perspective, the premise would be that in precolonial Africa what you had was communication. And then the impact of formal education, missionary intervention, one of the consequences was the creation of these various boxes called mother tongues that were the product of communication. So, in other words, mother tongues historically came after communication. And there's a lot of communication that takes place, but not necessarily through mother tongues. That's what I would say if I was put in a corner. Or if I put myself in your corner. That is why I find integrational linguistics compatible with colonial linguistics. Integrational linguistics enables me to talk about the communication that was existing in the context, in contexts in which there were no mother tongues.

**Hutton**

That can be very liberating.

**Makoni**

Yes, it enables me to say why it is that language planning and policies are always failing. They're always failing because they're trying to consider as natural artificial categories called mother tongues, when people interact through communication. Then the problem with the failures of the policies is not a matter of lack of resources or implementation. It's a conceptual problem. It doesn't matter how many resources you're going to throw at the problem, as long as conceptually you haven't resolved this ontological challenge between communication and language, that problem will keep manifesting itself at different stages throughout human history. That's the way I want to think about it. That's why I'm interested more and more in discussing the status of language or a language.

**Hutton**

People become stakeholders, don't they, in those languages.

**Makoni**

Yes.

**Hutton**

So, there's then, there is a tussle. Because they do take ownership of the labels and it may be the bargaining chip they have with the government in terms of resources or recognition.

**Madany-Saá**

Okay. We have another question in the chat by Dr Sangeeta Bagga-Gupta and I will ask Dr Sangeeta to read the question, one of which actually was somehow already answered about the mother construct.

**Sangeeta Bagga-Gupta (Jönköping University, Sweden)**

This was a very interesting read and it made me think or rethink about stuff I've done on the construct of mother tongue. You've already positioned yourself in terms of this construct being a European one. I have colleagues in Asia who use the concept mother tongue and that troubles me because they are using resources from five to six different named languages and, of course, this is a circulation of European constructs that come to different parts of the world. So, my question to you is what you write about Herder's 1772 construct, father and mother tongue: why did that not catch on? How was this transition in the 19th century, by Grimm, into mother tongue? What happened to father tongue? So that's one part. And the other is that isn't this construct a very monolingual one? And I particularly align with Sinfree's earlier comment on the ontological status of language (i.e. the need to conceptually consider the difference accorded to communication and language), which is key because unless we come to terms with what we are doing (with these concepts) we will continue to have neologisms coming up. I get the sense that mother or father tongue is something very central. Could you comment on these?

---

### Comments from the chat box

**Unyierie Idem (Holyoke Community College, USA):** In many African societies, the 'mother tongue' is actually the 'father tongue' – the language of one's father's ethnicity. In those patriarchal societies, children inherit or claim their father's language. Therefore, my mother tongue is Annang because Annang is my father's language. In homes where the mothers are of a different ethnicity, the children do not claim her language as their mother tongue. I guess my point is that the concept of mother tongue is fluid – it means different things to different groups.

    **Susan Coetzee-Van Rooy (North-West University, South Africa):** We name languages as subject at school in SA as home languages. And then kids can take a First Additional Language, Second Additional Language etc. So you are right... if you go to school you are already 'trained' about notions of home language and additional languages.

    **Unyierie Idem:** It is true that several languages may be used at home, but in the African societies I am referring to, the father's language is considered the mother tongue. In my case, I speak both my mother's and father's languages, but my father's is the mother tongue, not my mother's.

    **Susan Coetzee-Van Rooy:** Ah! Interesting, Unyierie! The participants I work with are also urban South Africans. So, these contexts differ. Thanks for explaining!

---

### Hutton

I don't have a good answer. I know that European romanticism is key in this because then you have this idealization of the bond between mother and child. The mother's milk, the language that you get with the mother's milk. So, this is one of these interesting concepts which, although they're feminized, they also have a very hard political edge. So, father tongue I discussed in terms of Jewish identity. At least from a certain point of view, Hebrew is a patriarchal language. So you have German antisemitism, which somehow mistrusts the Jewish model of identity, if I can generalise, which is from this nationalist point of view: 'Oh Jews can take on any nationality because they don't have deep-rooted loyalties and mother tongue, because their identity comes from a textual tradition and a religious tradition'. So here seems to be a bifurcation, some sort of problem for this sort of Protestant mother-tongue model, with the father Hebrew as the key language of identity for Jews. I agree entirely it's a monolingual idea because you must protect the bond. This is what Weisgerber is saying. The early childhood socialisation is when you form the basic and most effective concepts that make you a member of the *Volk*, and if there's some foreign father or the state language is foreign, then this is threatened. I think this is where this anxiety arises, because it's not a natural link. It's a quasi-natural link. It's not given in biology, it must be protected socially. That's where I see the anxieties around mother tongue and monolingualism. So, then you had all these studies showing that bilinguals have psychological, cognitive problems. So, you get a kind of psycholinguistics that follows from that. In Hong Kong, you hear people say 'Cantonese is the mother tongue of Hong Kong people'. The concept of mother tongue has been integrated into the politics of Hong Kong. I have difficulty in saying anything about that except there it is, there's this concept which has been integrated into the politics of this particular space. You can go back historically and say there is no notion of mother tongue in Chinese in premodernity... I challenged my colleagues in the Chinese department 'Can you find this concept?' and I don't think you can. But, nonetheless, it's now integral to Hong Kong. It's another of these problems of borrowing and so on. But anyway, yes, the father tongue. I think it could be discussed more. Because if you're German in the interwar period, if you're living outside the German state, and the language of the home is German but you're living in Poland, then the father language in the sense of state language is Polish and the school system and so on. So that's where you get this anxiety. But, nonetheless, it has politically devastating consequences because from the German nationalist point of view these states are threatening whole sections of the German people.

### Madany-Saá

Okay, we have the next question from Dr Judy Baker.

### Judith Baker (African Storybook Initiative of South Africa Institute for Distance Education)

Yes. Thank you very much. To me working on early child literacy, mother tongue becomes incredibly important, whatever you call it, because the language that the child acquires at home is such an enormous advantage to learning how to process text. And if you try to learn reading and writing, processing text in any other language than the one that you have all of the vocabulary and the visualisation and all that your brain contains, it becomes very hard to learn textual control. So, I just wanted to ask, how do we, you know, look at both mother tongue, language and translanguage from a political point of view, but also from a brain development point of view?

### Hutton

I think I said this in the book somewhere because I was aware of this: you really need to look very closely at the context. It would be ridiculous to say, you know, this concept is intrinsically fascistic or something. And I think there's perfect rationale to certain views of early language learning and childhood literacy. It's just that it struck me so hard reading that this idea basically in Nazi Germany is an antisemitic idea. It's hidden but once you think about it, it has such a hard political edge. But that doesn't mean that about the sort of practice you're talking about. It makes perfect sense what you said. So, I guess, this is why it's a difficult and challenging concept, I think, you know, it needs to be read in its political, social and pedagogical context. Because the notion of mother tongue is also a liberational concept, you know, it comes in the Reformation and so on. So it is against Latin, and expresses the idea that people should participate in their own institutions in a language of their socialisation. There's a strong liberal tradition to this idea as well. So that's why it's difficult to get one's head around it. I think, you know. I hope that's some kind of answer.

### Baker

Yeah. Thank you. Thank you. I just, it's just so hard when you talk to people when you're using something in many different ways. So, there's the anti-colonialist argument [which] is hugely important. It's also important in language learning and early acquisition. And then you want to switch over to a translanguaging frame. And it just seems to be that we don't have the actual language to make it clear to people. So, it's very easy to get confused.

### Hutton

I agree. I was thinking about, you know, when I came to Hong Kong there was a huge literature on how the education system, which is kind of mostly in English or the more high-status bits of it and a lot of students were struggling. So, there was a whole literature about how this was bad for cognitive development and so on. But now this literature has disappeared because the attitudes to English have completely changed in this society under the political pressures that it's under. You need to write a PhD to map this. I say to the students today, when I came to Hong Kong people were complaining bitterly about English in education and its cognitive effects, and they look at me blankly, because for them they've integrated English into their social identities and their political identities. This is a very complex postcolonial society which is evolving very rapidly. So, the arguments even about cognitive stuff fall away in a particular political context. Because students here don't have a problem, at least they don't write essays anymore saying what a pain it is to study in English and mother tongue would be better. That's just to emphasise that deeply contextual nature of this concept and what we say about it. Yeah, I agree entirely that translanguaging is problematic because, as Allan Bell said, people start off their articles for the journal *Language in Society* saying languages don't exist, then they go through the article using language names. We're in a very interesting moment, I think, in this, in this debate about the meta-language. What is the proper meta-language? And can there be or should there be one? And this is something I've been thinking about, you know, linguistics was originally trying to set up a universal meta-language and that goes into Fishman and Kloss. There's going to be a terminology you're going to apply to postcolonial states or decolonizing states globally so as to be able to diagnose. And then I think this fell apart, rightly so, actually. But then how do we think comparatively without a meta-language, so… I keep going round and around in my head about these issues.

## Makoni

Yes, I think I agree with you that, ultimately, it's a debate about the nature of the meta-language that we use. And I can see the problem, the dilemmas that translanguaging specialists find themselves in: languages don't exist or languages exist? And then when they encounter a piece of text and they go around naming those particular elements as Xhosa or Shona, etc. So, in part of the analysis they don't exist, then you're naming them using these particular categories. I think it's an issue about meta-language, and Peter Jones in a chapter that he wrote with Dorthe Duncker for one of my books extends this discussion to the notion of transcription. What you have with transcriptions as well is that people then transcribe these whatever conversations that people make and they end up with the impression, without being fully aware, that the transcription, whatever form it takes, is also in the process of creating a particular visual representation of language. But then the question is: can you do any analysis without some form of transcription? Or you have to do some transcription? Peter Jones and Dorthe Duncker, I think, write about transcription. But then the question is: if a graduate student were to ask you 'So what do I do? I mean, how do I handle this? How can I analyse this data if I don't transcribe it?' Unless you get it back and say, well, but there's nothing called data in terms of language. Then that's another different philosophical debate that you'd enter into. Mm hmm.

## Madany-Saá

Another very interesting question from Dr Cristine Severo about the right over mother tongue claimed by Indigenous peoples. Dr Severo, would you like to ask your question?

## Cristine Severo (Federal University of Santa Catarina, Brazil)

I will just follow-up on Professor Rajan's question. Can't we think of a kind of 'strategic essentialism' in relation to language when, for example, Indigenous peoples reclaim their right over their 'mother tongue' as part of a deep movement of identity affirmation and recognition? How would we consider the discourses on 'native languages' used by Indigenous to claim their dignity today? And I would also ask another question. If we consider the relation between colonialism, theology and religion, can't we think of this idea of mother tongue or native language as connected to Christianity or as a Christian invention? Since Latin was considered a sacred language and if you want to have access to truth, this access is just through sacred languages, like Latin. Thanks.

## Hutton

Yeah, thanks. I think, again, this is about the context that you look at. So, people who are in a particular historical situation need to use the tools that they have and some of these have been given to them or imposed on them. But, nonetheless, they are powerful tools because they also are recognisable within the sort of colonial or postcolonial national state. So, they're using categories, which were not originally in their Indigenous languages. Presumably. But, nonetheless, this is a way of transacting with the state in a way that's recognisable to the state. There are studies of these kinds of paradoxes that you get with the different forms of essentialisation that go on. Even, you know, with notions of ownership. This is key in relation to land. So, you may have assertions expressed in terms of a kind of ownership which would be foreign to the precolonial culture. But, nonetheless, within the legal order with which people find themselves, these make sense. Just like the Native American tribes. They can incorporate themselves as legal entities or they can use various legal forms in order to assert kinds of ownership over intellectual property and so on. So, that's why I say you really must be delicate about the context. First, the missionaries come and say you have this mother tongue. Then you have some people say, actually, it's a complete construct, you know. That would be appalling and ridiculous. And I think there are good reasons behind this. These are very powerful ideas and once they enter society, they can be used in many different ways. And so, it's not for me to say what people should do with these concepts. It's just that I, working from the one context that I was looking at, it was kind of a shock to me. So, on the issue of mother tongue you have the Reformation, which is exactly a rebellion against the notion that an institution should mediate, in a language you can't understand, between you and God. That is maybe not discussed enough in the history of linguistics, because this is such a profound revolution. So, then you have Luther, the Bible translation, and so on, saying I don't need necessarily a caste of priests and a Pope to mediate between me and God. Of course, you end up creating a high variety of German, so a kind of a church German, but so you don't get a complete levelling. I guess in parts of the world the first missionaries were Jesuits, but they also did linguistics. You have this in China, which I know a bit better, where you have the early Catholic missionaries going to the elite of the society and trying to convert from the top. And you have radical Protestants in the 19th century who sounded like Marxists, who were saying that the writing system is elitist and we need to use vernacular and dialect, and you need to write the Bible in Latin letters. So, they can teach someone to read the Bible in a few weeks in a Romanized Chinese. So, it's a radical technology, and it is empowering in a sense, and girls and women get educated by missionaries. There's a whole set of difficult issues there, I think, which defeat me because I just go round in circles. But yes, the point is well taken, that these concepts that circulate globally can be appropriated, adapted and can become meaningful, yes. And they can be used to resist different attempts to level or wipe out or attack particular cultures. We're cursed with the wider frame and this historical awareness of things, I guess. That reflexivity which makes everything much more difficult.

## Madany-Saá

We have so many more questions. Ashraf, would you like to ask your question?

## Ashraf Abdelhay (Doha Institute for Graduate Studies, Qatar)

Thank you so much, Professor Hutton. I take issue with the way translanguaging is used in some writings. My understanding is that translanguaging, the way it's used now in the literature, eradicates or conflates practice with ideology. Because, as I understand translanguaging, it focuses on processes and practices of meaning making. The question is: where does ideology fit? There's no talk about it. I think this is a problem which we need to address. The second thing is that when you say 'language' doesn't exist. Who's the audience for this statement? It can't be the man or woman on the street. It could be the linguist and I think it is the linguist. We are trying to do battle within the field saying to our colleagues that 'language', in the way that it's reified, doesn't exist in the street. But I think the problem here is that we have taken this debate to the street and we are saying to people language doesn't exist. 'You're translanguaging!' You can't say to your mother 'You're translanguaging, mother' or to your friend 'You're just translanguaging'. So, I think we need to deal with the problem of metalanguage, their function and audience, etc. For me, translanguaging as a metalanguage is the dear companion to colonial linguistics. In this way, the questions of ideology and power relations are addressed when the concept of 'translanguage' is used as a tool of critique of the modernist conception of language. The second point is the notion of mother tongue in the oral tradition. I have tried to look for this term in the Arabic tradition and it doesn't exist. Mother tongue as a phrase is imported from the West into Arabic linguistics. And, interestingly, it was reconceptualised in local practice and linked with the standard. Thus, delinked from race when Standard Arabic is seen as a 'mother tongue'. Thus, this ideological dynamic has to be taken into account when we theorise the notion of mother tongue outside the Western tradition of linguistics. The last point is about native language. The concept of native language is not synonymous with the concept of mother tongue. This concept is also linked somehow with the notion of the modern nation state. Can you elaborate on these points, please?

## Hutton

I'm not sure about the translanguaging, I have to defer to others on that because I've noticed there's an explosion of literature, but I'm sure you have a point there. But I do very much agree with you about your second point. I remember going home to see my father and saying 'There's this professor at Oxford, he says languages don't exist' and my father looked to me like 'You guys up there in Oxford are wasting your time'. And he had a point! But Harris, actually, at least rhetorically did say that lay speakers, ordinary speakers, have the only concept of language worth having. So, exactly as you said, linguists have made these a kind of specialised currency. And it sits uneasily with these ordinary concepts which circulate socially. I still think there's a problem there, because who's a lay speaker? And where do lay ideas come from?

And who is to critique? That's why... back to... it'd be ridiculous for me to go to an Indigenous people and say 'You guys, your language is a construct', you know, which they are clinging on to. So, I think I've become more and more interested in that, actually, in relation to law, where you have judges, linguists, you know, you have all these people who are trying to work out what words mean and arguing about who has a better theory of what words mean. And it actually has practical consequences. And I think we should think more about the social circulation of linguistic ideas. Obviously, people go through formal education and they come out with what Harris would call the language myth, there are nouns and verbs, there's grammatical structures, words have meanings and so on. So, I do fear there's a danger of romanticising ordinary speakers as well: they live in a pre-categorical world of, you know, and so I, I think there's a lot to think about in your point there. And nation state... it's again back to the Reformation. So, you have the idea of authentic membership in an institution or a state. That's why Germany is so important because Germany had a language before it had a state. So, people, in a way, were members of the German *Volk* before they were citizens of a German state. There's something so powerful about this idea, this again romantic idea of integration into a kind of organic unity. This is the vernacular idea of nationalism. And of course, it has a liberational side again, because it means that the language of government is the language of the home or the language of school. At least it's some variant of the language of home. And that sounds more liberal, democratic and that's the argument for Protestantism, in a way.

You know, Bauman and Briggs have this discussion about, there's also a coercive or purifying moment where the nation state creates a kind of pure variety and marginalises. So, Germany, you know, was massively, in our terms, multi-ethnic, multi-cultural. The pre-modern... the sort of German state as it was in the late 18th and 19th century, the German territories, you know, it was full of all kinds of languages and varieties. And then you get this concept reified of German and Standard German imposed onto it. But I guess this model of a nation state became more and more powerful with the breakup of these large European empires. For example, the Austro-Hungarian empire. So, we're still living with the consequences also of the Ottoman Empire. One of the things that broke these empires was the idea of mother tongue or nation states, you know, based on language or culture. Not only, but this is one of the aspects of it.

I think this is, you know, one of the most important ideas in modern history and of course colonialism exports the idea of a particular model of nationalism, the nation state, which has proved highly problematic, obviously, not just in Europe, but everywhere. You have China, which is still basically an imperial polity, and it dealt with the internal variation by reifying people into different nationalities. It's as if Turkey was the Ottoman Empire. That's China, you know. Did I answer your question or...? Please follow up if you... for the translanguaging, I don't have a good answer for it.

### Abdelhay

My argument is that the notion of translanguaging, in the ways it's used, depoliticises linguistics. Because it divorces, actually it eradicates or puts under erasure, the whole notion of ideology. People just focus on practice, but what about ideology? And here they focus on ideology as it's used in professional linguistics, but they forget to focus on folk ideologies outside the western world. For example, take the notion of diglossia in the work of Charles Ferguson. They say 'Well, Ferguson got it wrong because we translanguage, it's not high and low'. But again, Ferguson paid attention to the notion of ideology. The idea of the singular language is there in the mind of the speaker and it remains to be seen where it comes from. There is a chapter by Suleiman titled 'Arabic Folk Linguistics: Between Mother Tongue and Native Language' in *The Oxford Handbook of Arabic Linguistics* edited by Jonathan Owens. You see what I mean? And this leads us to your point on lexicography and on your dictionary on the country's slang. It's very interesting. It seems like you're doing battle against the establishment to write a dictionary on slang, on the language of the street. So, what's the point behind that? I am asking because the notion of slang somehow links to the notion of mother tongue.

### Hutton

It's the same thing as I have today. I was frustrated because I was trying to learn Cantonese and all the words that I had around me I couldn't find in a dictionary. It's still a painful process. You know, it's still bound up with this huge political argument debate. There's a massive amount of linguistic creativity going on, but the lexicographers are nowhere near catching up with it. So, I started making a list in my office as the days go by. I'm sitting here. And I don't know if I'll publish it, but I just was so struck by the dynamism of the vernacular, yes this incredibly complex, especially with the social media. Unbelievable. What's going on in what would be called translanguaging, in the sort of mixing. But I understood translanguaging right, they think of themselves as political, right. I mean, I get the affect coming from translanguaging as... it does seem to be situating itself politically or am I wrong, Ashraf?

### Abdelhay

I think it's a controversial issue. They try to say, you know, that Western linguistics has constructed or created language and imposed it on a non-Western context and that's right, particularly in the colonial period. But the way now it's used to do research in non-Western contexts actually, as I see it, is seriously depoliticising research, you know. The argument of translanguaging emerged in the contexts where autonomous, mainstream Western linguistics dominate to inspect the nature of actual linguistic practice but now it's used in non-Western contexts. And the question of ideology is absent in the emerging research works in the Arab world which use the concept as an analytic tool. Some researchers now are saying: 'Well, since people are translanguaging, the notion of a singular language is not there'. Full stop. So, as I understand it, translanguaging emerged as a tool of resistance against the mainstream understanding of language in the Western theory. But now it's used to do violence when it's used in this way in other non-Western contexts.

## Hutton

I see your point. Yeah. Because it's missing out the folk models, the actual people. Folk, not in a dismissive sense, but actually in notions of language which are including hierarchies and standards and so on.

## Abdelhay

Yes. The folk ideologies of language. That's precisely what I meant.

## Madany-Saá

Okay, let's continue. We don't have much time. There's a really interesting conversation going on in the chat and there are still many questions about translanguaging. Maybe I will pick up the one by Eunjeong Lee. There were some comments about your question too, would you like to ask your question?

## Eunjeong Lee (University of Texas, USA)

The way that I understand translanguaging, I cannot really speak for everybody because it has been more or less an interdisciplinary discussion that has evolved in education, also composition and rhetoric as well as applied linguistics. It's important to understand that your positionality and whose work you're referring to also define or shape how you understand translanguaging. My understanding of translanguaging comes from work by Ofelia García and Ricardo Otheguy and also some of the literacy scholars in composition and rhetoric like Bruce Horner and also Suresh Canagarajah, who's an applied linguist. The way that I understand translanguaging is really about the positionality and epistemology as a multilingual and I have to slightly disagree with the idea that translanguaging may overlook folk ideology of language. Actually, to me, translanguaging really tries to highlight the idea that it is built upon the perspective of bilinguals who grow up, engage, navigate or work around the very idea of named language categories. So, in that sense, I don't think the scholars who have been advancing translanguaging frameworks disregard the idea of named language categories or even monolingual ideologies. Actually, they're trying to claim the very fact that we live with the consequence of language ideology. One way that people live with that ideology is that they feel very afraid to translanguage, but also there's a group of people who grow up actually contesting the boundaries. So that's how I understand translanguaging.

---

### Comments from the chat box

**Anna De Fina (Georgetown University, USA):** Plus the idea of resources rather than languages alone and those include other semiotic elements.

**Susan Coetzee-Van Rooy (North-West University, South Africa):** I also like the 2015 article by Ofelia and Otheguy. I like the point they make that links to what Sinfree said just now. Linguists are free to use meta-language; but we need to remember that people make meaning with socially agreed-on labels like isiXhosa. To ask them about how they translanguage would not make sense. To ask about the languages that they know and how they use them make sense. We need to respect the discourses of linguists about the thing they study and what people use to make meaning is not necessarily the same.

### Hutton

There's always this problem that the moment you enter linguistic analysis, you're moving into becoming an outsider. I mean, maybe Ashraf would like to respond, but I do think there's a fascinating and intricate problem about the inside or outside of categories and the different forms of ideology. You know, what you're saying back and forth with Ashraf would be an interesting dialogue about thinking about this. Because I do think for the history of linguistics, there's an assumption of the expert until, you know, which I think is that of an expert with a method that was the model. I think that now it's being questioned, anthropologically, and that's very healthy. This is a kind of a weak response to what you said.

### Abdelhay

Can I add something here just to make myself clear? If the notion of language is an ideological construct and if, as Christopher said, formal education leaves as its traces this ideological understanding of language, then translanguaging should not imply the absence of the referential conception of language. If the notion of language as a singular exists, it does exist at a particular level of reality even though we are, at another level, translanguaging. That reality can be an imagination; it can be a language myth in the folk ideology of the person on the street. It, however, shapes our choices, for example, in the case of which school to send our kids. To put it crudely, at the level of practice, the idea of the linguistic boundary is not there. But at the level of ideological imagination in the mind of the person on the street, it could be there. The question is how to reveal it, how to explore it, how to study it. The notion of translanguaging as a metalinguistic tool erases that possibility because we go for our research with the idea that there is no ideology because people just translanguage, we just focus on practice, and we then come out with an ideology-blind description of that practice. So, that level of reality, which is in the social mind, is systematically erased through the metalanguage of the research itself. Translanguaging, to reiterate, becomes a powerful decolonial tool when it is used within the frames of colonial linguistics and Southern theories, as some of us are now using it in this way. Otherwise, the questions of language ideologies and social justice are the obvious victims of its erasure. That's my point.

## Lee

As I said, I don't think translanguaging scholars would necessarily deny that we live with the consequence of monolingual ideology, one of which is the category of named language. I mean, given my current understanding of this evolving scholarship, what I think the scholars are highlighting is the effect of monolingual ideologies and what we have to deal with as bi-/multilinguals vs. how we actually live with and across different named languages and ideologies and one of which is translanguaging. And I think that says something about how we want to see the reality and from whose perspective. Because, as we discussed, there are multiple perspectives, there are linguists who label language and describe language and name things, but that is one perspective. What I find translanguaging helpful for is that the framework helps us to push back that that's not the only perspective in understanding our linguistic realities. And, in doing so, I see that there is a potential risk of perhaps minimising the actual reality where people feel the pressure of monolingual ideology differently in terms of our representation. I can see that. But the framework itself, again, shows us that it comes down upon our responsibility as a scholar to make it clear where you stand in terms of using that framework and to what end. And, by doing so, whose perspective you are foregrounding.

## Madany-Saá

Thank you very much, Eunjeong. We already reached our 90 minutes of discussion time so probably some of you already have some other plans. However, as I mentioned before, I will stop recording, but I know that we still have some questions in the chat. So, if you wish to stay for some more minutes, for an informal part of the session, you're very welcome to do so. Thank you so much everyone for your inspiring questions and thank you so much Dr Hutton for your participation. If you just read in the chat there are many warm words of gratitude for your participation today.

## Hutton

Thank you. I'm really grateful. I mean, I've been sort of isolated the last few weeks. Wonderfully exciting to have a sort of global conversation like this, that's really great, the corridor is empty today. We have a new virus wave.

## References

Harris, R. and Hutton, C. (2007) *Definition in Theory and Practice: Language, Lexicography and the Law.* London: Continuum.

Heller, M. and McElhinny, B. (2017) *Language, Capitalism, Colonialism: Toward a Critical History.* Toronto: University of Toronto Press.

Hutton, C. (1999) *Linguistics and the Third Reich: Mother-tongue Fascism, Race and the Science of Language.* London: Routledge

Hutton, C. (2005) *Race and the Third Reich: Linguistics, Racial Anthropology and Genetics in the Dialectic of Volk.* Cambridge: Polity Press.

Hutton, C. (2009) *Language, Meaning and the Law*. Edinburgh: Edinburgh University Press.
Hutton, C. (2019a) *Integrationism and the Self: Reflections on the Legal Personhood of Animals*. London: Routledge.
Hutton, C. (2019b) *The Tyranny of Ordinary Meaning: Corbett v Corbett and the Invention of Legal Sex*. Cham: Palgrave.
Owens, J. (ed.) (2019) *The Oxford Handbook of Arabic Linguistics*. Oxford: Oxford University Press.
Weinreich, U. (1953) *Languages in Contact: Findings and Problems*. New York: Linguistic Circle of New York.

# 3 Struggle, Voice, Justice: A Conversation and Some Words of Caution about the Sociolinguistics We Hope For

Monica Heller and Bonnie McElhinny

**Rafael Lomeu Gomes**

I would like to welcome everyone and introduce the special guests for the session today, Monica Heller and Bonnie McElhinny, who have kindly agreed to participate in our session to discuss their book *Language, Capitalism, Colonialism: Toward a Critical History*, published in 2017 by the University of Toronto Press.

Monica Heller was born and raised in Montréal (Québec). She did her post-secondary education in the United States and has spent her career at the University of Toronto, with stints of various lengths in Europe and Latin America. A past president of the American Anthropological Association, she currently chairs the Royal Society of Canada's Committee on Public Engagement. She has received honorary doctorates from the Universität Bern (Switzerland) and the Université de Bretagne Occidentale (France). Her research has focused on the role of language in the making of social difference and social inequality, with a focus on shifting ideologies of nationalism (particularly in francophone North America) and on shifting ideologies of language in late capitalism.

Bonnie McElhinny is Principal of New College at the University of Toronto, and Professor of Anthropology and Women and Gender Studies. She is the former Director of Women and Gender Studies. She regularly teaches courses on unsettling settler colonialism, living on the water in Toronto, and water and social justice. She directs Water Allies @ New College, with the support of a Faculty of Arts and Science Teaching and Learning Grant. This initiative focuses on decolonial, feminist, queer and anti-racist approaches to environmental justice, with a focus on water. Its projects include designing and re-designing a cluster of courses on the Great Lakes, research and teaching collaborations with community partners, designing experiential learning opportunities for students, and curating public events.

I have a couple of questions that I'd like to ask you for us to start. The first one is connected to a reflection that you make in the preface of the book on radical hope, which I find very inspiring. And perhaps one of the reasons I find it so inspiring is because it's very timely but also atemporal. A comment that you make is that you draw on Arendt's work and also on Junot Diaz and you mention the number of years apart of both contributions, and both touch on the issue of hope. I was inspired to use it in my own teaching as well, right after we transitioned to online modes of teaching at the University of Oslo due to the coronavirus pandemic. I wanted to start a conversation with our students to check in with them how they were coping and I was interested in sharing with them the idea of radical hope as an everyday life strategy, as mentioned in your book. And I wanted to read more about Junot Diaz, whose work I didn't know and this, like I said, was in the wake of the pandemic. And I believe, as many of you, I had to make very quick plans to adapt so I started reading more about Junot Diaz. I came across some pieces on the news covering how he faced allegations of sexual abuse and harassment, that had some implications to some positions that he held, and I started to think 'Okay, so what do I do from here?'. In a way, it connects to a point that you make in your book when you talk about the history of sociolinguistics, and here I'm using scare quotes, the 'founders' of sociolinguistics, how Dell Hymes also met allegations of sexual harassment. And I wasn't sure exactly whether I should cite Diaz without entering this history that I know little about, but still wanted to inspire students to find radical hope as a strategy for their, or our, everyday lives. So, I was wondering if you could perhaps talk a little bit about radical hope and the politics of citation.

## Bonnie McElhinny

First of all, I just want to thank all of you for participating in this conversation. I approach this conversation with a great deal of humility, knowing all that I can learn from the people that are in this room and regretting, in many ways, that we are interacting in this way rather than person-to-person, so that we'd have the opportunity for more robust conversations. I also want to flag that we're speaking from a historic moment where we're facing multiple crises, and I want to reflect on that. I know that this can be a disembodied form of interaction, but this is a moment where we are thinking concretely and more forcibly than ever before or again about how to challenge anti-Black violence, how to think about policing, how we deepen our commitment to anti-racist and decolonial work. That is very much part of the conversation I'm engaged in right now at the University of Toronto. The College I'm principal of supports programs in African Studies, Caribbean Studies, Critical Studies in Equity and Solidarity, Buddhist Psychology and Mental Health. We're reflecting both on the work done, and the work we have yet to do.

We're also speaking from this moment of global pandemic, where I'm listening to each of you, as we opened up, describing the moments... the ways in which you are grappling. Life is harder now, with whatever sets of circumstances you are facing. We're seeing at the moment the diagnosis, what we need to attend to, what we haven't attended to. It helps us diagnose what matters. And that is a somber moment, I think it's a somber moment. It is also a moment of hope. It's a moment, where, as I talked to colleagues at the College, we were thinking about grief and healing, and organizing. And trying to find the right balance between those.

I won't speak for Monica, because, actually, Monica and I have had sustained discussions about the notion of hope and we might want to speak to that, because we debated about whether to put notions of hope in the book. So, from my perspective, I need not just to be able to say no. Naomi Klein, who is a socialist writer based in British Columbia, has a book called *No Is Not Enough* published in 2017 by Alfred A. Knopf Canada. It's not enough for me to say this is what we're not doing, we cannot do, what we can no longer do. I also need the vision of what we're working towards. And for me hope is about that. Hope is having a vision of what we're working towards. Hope is also finding the moments where we are already instantiating that future in our ongoing interactions even if briefly. So, I wanted to think about hope. I also think that without notions of hope we might get stuck in the status quo and that's ultimately a conservative position.

So, as we were finishing the book, it was another somber moment. It was a moment when Trump had just been elected President of the United States, and we were just finishing the preface. And we knew that that was going to be a very challenging moment where fascist ideas, racist ideas, colonial ideas would have a proponent in one of the most powerful offices in the world. Junot Diaz had written an article in *The New Yorker* the week after Trump was elected where he drew on Jonathan Lear's ideas of radical hope to note that the work has never been easy and it will not be easy, and for us the quote spoke to the moment. At that point, the critique of some of Diaz's sexist actions had not become public, it became public after.

Rafael, I have a couple of responses to your specific question. One is: I still want to draw on the notion of hope and, for the work I do because I'm not working on Dominican literature, I don't need to draw on Junot Diaz to do that. He draws on Jonathan Lear himself. In our final chapter, we have a section called 'This Is How We Hope'. We draw on a number of scholars – socialist scholars, feminist scholars, queer scholars, scholars imagining Indigenous and Black futurities – who elaborate notions of hope, vision and optimism. And I think that's what I would do at this moment. If we have another edition at some point we might have to speak exactly to the question that Rafael asked. So, I would call the names of Sara Ahmed, Lauren Berlant, José Muñoz, Leanne Simpson, Sylvia Wynter, Angela Davis, Stefano Harney, Fred Moten, Karyn Recollet. Some of these names are probably names that circulate globally. But others are scholars here in this place in Toronto or southern Ontario or in Canada, who are doing the work on the ground. I think that it's appropriate to have that mix. So yes, I think we need hope. The question of citing Hymes and what it means to have to grapple with our own tradition is maybe the moment at which I'll tip over to Monica and we can flip back if we need to.

## Monica Heller

I'm not the hope person. We had a lot of discussions about this. It has a lot to do also with my own family background. I don't need an actual vision. I need to be in the struggle. I guess I talk a lot about rethinking and re-imagining but I don't think of that as prior to the everyday life work of trying to be true to the certain values and trying to make them real in some way. So, I fully expect and I've certainly had the experience of failing regularly and that's fine.

I want there to be a conversation, I want there to be a space for a conversation, I want to be able to struggle. I reconciled myself to the notion of hope through that. I guess that's my version of it. But the word often makes me nervous because I worry that it can tip over too easily into various notions of utopia, which have their own potentials for terror, for domination, for things that are the antithesis of the world that I want to be living in.

I think there's lots of different ways to do this and I prefer a broader range with maybe other kinds of more processual terminologies. I think it's possible to retain that energy for struggle, remembering that it is also fine to be really exhausted and have to go home and rest for a while and recharge because otherwise you just can't do it. The trick in many ways is to be able to be attentive to when you need to withdraw from battle for a moment and allow that to happen.

Another thing about hope is to ask who is doing the talking about it. This is one of the reasons why I think it's important to think about why we cite people. And the concern I think that I certainly had with Hymes is that he is cited for notions like narrative inequality as someone who was attentive to questions of inequality and power in the field. But, in his personal practice, he contradicted that in ways which produced concrete results for the field, which were the antithesis of what we thought he was imagining. So, voices were silenced through his actions, which is perhaps the essence of narrative inequality. So, I'm not going to cite Hymes as someone who inspires me on that notion.

In addition, in the book we wanted to avoid 'the great person view' of intellectual history, intellectual genealogies. There are lots of people in these conversations. With citational practices we do need to be careful about the ideas and how they come through particular personal histories, and through what we do with the construction of the person as opposed to the construction of the ideas. I'm not trying to say that it's the work that matters, not the person. On the contrary, and I think that the entire way in which we constructed our book is about that. But rather that if the idea is something that inspires us, there's a lot of work that we can do to work on that idea without attributing it uncritically to people who are then constructed as heroes in the cause. We can't know everything about everybody and that's fine. I think what it turns around for me is to think about what the struggle is like for me and how to be attentive to the consequences of my own practices, and learn from them, and allow myself to make mistakes. But to make an attempt at least at some kind of consistency and coherence.

## Sinfree Makoni

Yes, Bonnie and Monica, thank you very much for agreeing to come and talk to us about your book. I read your book when me and Alastair Pennycook were writing our book called *Innovations and Challenges to Applied Linguistics from the Global South* which was published in 2019 by Routledge. I reread it again in preparation for this particular discussion.

So, the questions I'm going to raise are grounded in my interpretation of your work, not as reflected in the book that we wrote, but as reflected in the discussion after we had finished writing our own book. What I found striking about your work was the extent to which the other parts of the globe were more or less silent. I understand you said in the beginning that you're writing from Canada and the United States, but viewing sociolinguistics and aspects about colonialism outside North America the world seems to be very different. In other words, what I'm asking is what does sociolinguistics look like outside the North American space? Because your main interest in writing is to move towards a critical history of language colonialism and capitalism. So, my question is what does it look like from the other side of the world?

### Heller

I'll try to respond. I'm not going to answer because that's not a question I can answer. We actually didn't arrive at the title until the very end of the process. And we were actually initially asked to write an introductory textbook for linguistic anthropology and an accompanying reader. We didn't want to do that, and it took us a while to figure out why. We kind of did a bait-and-switch and went back to UT Press and said 'We don't want to do what you asked us to do. We want to do something different'. Because, for us, the textbook format is canonical. It defines a field without situating itself. And we had been feeling for a while that there were a lot of questions that we had that we couldn't ask within the framework of the field that we had been socialized into and were practicing. We felt we had to rethink a lot of things in order to be able to arrive at some other way of asking questions. So, I hope that we were clear that in writing this book we're not trying to define the field. We're not trying to make a definitive statement. What we're trying to do is to open up a way of thinking broadly about the relationship between communicative meaning-making and social processes in which issues of power and inequality are centered rather than carved off in some way. And to suggest that there's lots of different ways in which we enter this set of conversations. We don't know them all for obvious reasons. And it seemed that the best way in which we could enter this conversation was from how we got into it, our voices, so that we can enter into conversation with you.

### Makoni

Right, that's fair. So let me then continue with my thoughts. In the book, in a very tantalizing way and I think I agree with you, you say that there are certain notions about language, which at times may look liberatory, but they may end up being repressive. And there are some that may begin as repressive, and then may be used for new political purposes. And I was asking myself: What are the concrete examples that you had in mind when you were talking about how certain notions about language, which may initially begin as liberatory, but may end up as repressive and some may begin as repressive but may end up being liberatory? What specific notions about language did you have in mind?

## McElhinny

Sinfree Makoni, if I can speak to your last question and this one. Because it's an important question that you're asking. There's no one book, there's no one book. There should not be one book that speaks to all of the different historical positions and trajectories. So, we are situated, the two of us are, as we noted in the introduction, in a powerful peripheral position with respect to the American Empire.

We're in Canada. We are both American trained. I'm American and also now Canadian. We are both White. And there are certain kinds of questions we felt we needed to ask as people who are in the center of one powerful empire, the American Empire, and also in another powerful country, a settler colonial state: Canada. And we were excavating the tradition that shapes our work, which is in the ways of empire a kind of voracious one, right? There are ways in which work that's happening within other traditions is picked up. There are other parts of those traditions that are ignored. And there are parts of it that are ventriloquized and not properly cited, right? You take it up and the work is taken to be the work of scholars from the empire when, in fact, the work happened elsewhere.

So, what we were trying to think a bit about was what happens in the elaboration of ideas at the center of this American Empire and Canadian settler colonial nation. For us, one example would be the tradition of phonetics... the history of that is written as an innovation, a scientific innovation that started in Britain in the 19th century. But that work was elaborated in complex and rich conversation with the traditions for analyzing language in India at the time and they were part of that colonial conversation. Some of those conversations were obscured. The long contributions of the Sanskrit tradition were obscured.

We've argued, too, in the book that in the 1960s a number of American sociolinguists, who are part of these big development schemes, are sent to a range of sites in the world, and again India is one of them. John Gumperz, William Bright, a number of people who are often associated with the American sociolinguistic tradition and have powerful positions in that tradition did work in India. Sometimes what happens is that the scholarly traditions are erased in the ways those stories are retold such that they were seemed to be inspired by their fieldwork rather than by exchanges with scholars and scholarly traditions. Gumperz would say it was the sociolinguistic traditions, not just the communities that he encountered, that inspired him. But that work of erasure and reframing is partly what we're trying to show. And we are trying to show the ways that certain kinds of traditions that are articulated in some of the areas that are colonized by the US... though like work on creoles that is coming out of Hawaiʻi and the work on pidgins and creoles coming out of the Caribbean are critical, they're very important sites. They're key sites for thinking about decolonial work, antiracist work for challenging existing traditions (for example, the notion of a linguistic family tree and thus what a family means).

But that work is often kind of off to the side or in parallel traditions, it's not centered fully. And we were trying to make sense of the kinds of questions we could not ask. Why it is so tough to ask certain kinds of questions that are critical of capitalism? What happened in the American Empire to make questions around political economy hard to ask? And that Cold War chapter is us looking at the active suppression of intellectuals and ideas. And those were the progressive intellectuals of the time. They were mostly White, they were mostly male, a number of them were Jewish.

So that's who was in the American academy at the time. But those folks were asking questions about anti-Semitism. They were asking questions, critiquing ideas about miscegenation. They were asking questions about anti-Black racism. They were asking, in a certain way, questions about indigeneity. Some of them were working on Indigenous languages. And those voices were written out. They were either taken right out of the academy, or drummed out of the Academy. Or their voices, you know, were silenced because they received so much critique (see someone like Melville Jacobs). So, we are looking at how an empire polices its intellectual tradition and creates it, knowing full well that what that requires then is that we need to know more of those histories as they're told not from the empire, but from the global South. But also understanding that the global South is in the empire. Indigenous nations are created as dependents within the empire, but it's not the way the nations so understand themselves.

So, some of those voices that we draw on are Indigenous voices from this place. We talk about the water walkers. We cite a number of Indigenous scholars because those are the scholars who are speaking back from what is construed by the settler colonial state as 'within' but by them as 'without'... I'm very interested in thinking about the solidarities that emerge between subaltern groups in different sites. And I think that's going to be an exciting conversation. And that the people in this room are already... Sinfree, your book and then other people in this room are building those conversations. So that's exciting and I'm going to be just sitting back and learning.

## Makoni

When I was preparing for this particular session, I was reading your book together with the book by Raewyn Connell, *Southern Theory* (the one published in 2007 by Polity Press) in an attempt to see how I could frame my arguments about your work from that particular southern theoretical perspective. And towards the last part of her book, she talks about something that is similar to what we're discussing now: the importance of analyzing the local intellectual traditions in different parts of the world and at times looking at the nature of the relationships between the different peripheral systems, let's say, Southern Africa, Brazil and Australia etc. to see how ideas circulate in those different places. OK. But let me ask you another question, then I will open the discussion. Since you are interested in dealing with Indigenous communities, where does the issue of land fit in in your notion of sociolinguistics?

## Heller

I think the issue is how to imagine a set of conversations in which we see things radically differently but can still talk to each other, right? So, in that sense, again, I don't think we are after a theory of sociolinguistics, right? We're after, or I'm after,

I'll speak for myself, a way of understanding that there are all kinds of different ways and all kinds of different fields in which ideas circulate that are consequential for all of us. So, part of the job is to understand how power works, and one of the things that we sidle away from, that sociolinguistics as an institutionalized global North field has sidled away from, is understanding the workings of power and what is erased as a result. But there are also ways in which sometimes the dominant fields need to shut up and listen, right? To not assume the enlightenment universal frame for everybody. But, rather, maybe more helpfully, one can think about how to make bridges across positions – ways of understanding the world, ways of being in the world – which are radically different from each other for excellent and understandable reasons, which don't necessarily need to be subsumed under one. But relationship to the land, to water, to air, I mean to the material world is certainly something that we have in common. We think about it differently. The issue for me is: what are the consequences of the ways in which we think about it, not just for us, but for everybody else that we live with?

## Busi Makoni (Pennsylvania State University, USA)

My question is about the issue of citation. I noticed that the preoccupation, at least in sociolinguistics, is to discuss the issues around Hymes, whether to cite him or not to cite him.

Why is that very important? An issue that then gets sidelined in the process is the citation of Black women scholars whether African Americans or Africans. I have noticed over the years that, in citational practices, the tendency is to focus on White women writing in the West rather than citing other scholars. If you cite other scholars writing outside the US, or who are Black, or even those writing in the West who are non-White, you are often reminded during the review process that the individuals cited are unknown: 'Why don't you cite so, and so, and so, and so?' Often those are the big names of White women in the West. It seems as if the acknowledgment of Black women's intellectual production is often not a central issue in our scholarship. In so doing, it comes across as if spaces of knowledge production do silence and erase Black women from the academy. Even here, we have just talked about Dell Hymes, but that's part of issues related to Black women. Even in feminist scholarship, it's the same practice. So, I would like Monica and Bonnie to comment on how they see this.

## McElhinny

I appreciate your question. I did a study a few years ago on citational practices in the field. We analyzed five journals and it was published in a journal in which citation practices of women came out looking relatively strong. We were looking at the politics of citation. How is theory constructed? Who is seen as theoretical? Whose voices are cited? In one section in the book we draw on Marcyliena Morgan's work on Claudia Mitchell-Kernan. Marcyliena Morgan is an African American woman, a scholar who describes the way that, for her, Claudia Mitchell-Kernan was a key early figure in thinking about sociolinguistics. One of the earliest Black women scholars in the field. And yet, her work is often not cited in the histories of the field. Morgan talks about the ways that the reviews of her early work dismissed Mitchell-Kernan in part because she was of the community, and were quite explicit in their sexist comments. And so, she looks at that erasure as she rewrites another version of the history. I think that's a call to all of us to think about who are centering in our discussions as theoretical. And once we get started, we are not done. Sometimes people find one person, maybe they find Marcyliena Morgan or maybe they find Claudia Mitchell-Kernan and that person then becomes *the* person, and that's a problematic practice, as well.

So, the framing of our book is deliberate in saying we were talking about walking backwards into the future, and we have four theoretical frameworks. One is Raymond Williams, a socialist scholar who comes from another periphery, Wales, a powerful periphery. And he is thinking about socialist work, and he has certain lacunae. Edward Said has noted the ways in which his form of socialism is not attentive to the role that Britain has as a colonial power when he writes about city and country; he has certain things to contribute, and he has certain lacunae. We draw on Said's work on Orientalism, as he also has class and gender lacunae.

We draw on Sylvia Wynter, who is a Black Caribbean-based scholar and artist, who is seen as central in many discussions here in Canada because of the ways in which she is thinking about reimagining what human is, reimagining relationships between Indigeneity and Blackness. And because she also uses a theoretical framework that is about narrative.

The final theoretical perspective is drawn from Indigenous women, and this circles back to Makoni's question about land. There's an Anishinaabe elder, Josephine Mandamin, who about a decade and a half ago, started walking around each of the Great Lakes. The Great Lakes contain 20% of the world's freshwater, so these are month-long journeys, and she was in her sixties. She started to walk around the Great Lakes and, at first, it was just herself and her sister. She walked it and it was a way of reclaiming. Reclaiming knowledge of the place, reclaiming names where English names had been laminated on. She walked around each of the lakes and as she walked more and more people started to walk with her. Other people started to do water walks. They were led largely by Indigenous women around other water bodies. Her last walk was in her mid-eighties and she started in Minnesota and she walked around each of the Great Lakes, the whole way around the Great Lakes and then out the Saint Lawrence Seaway. It's her story to tell. There are videos of her describing the things that she learned, the things she picked up along the way, and what it means to take that and imagine a different kind of future.

But those were, those are four theoretical perspectives that for us framed the work. I don't claim to know all that I need to know. But this is one of the moments where I'm thinking about where do I draw inspiration, not, you know from theoretical work and ethnographic work, and then that kind of rewriting of history that Marcyliena Morgan is offering. So, what would it mean to center Claudia Mitchell-Kernan and our understanding of the origin of sociolinguistics in the 1960s in the United States instead of Hymes, Gumperz and Labov. How does that change our sense of what the central questions should be?

## Heller

She's [Mitchell-Kernan] an interesting case. I mean, she's one of those cases which links up to the interest that we had in the Social Science Research Council Committee on Sociolinguistics. Since she is someone who was mentioned as somebody who could be invited and yet somehow never was.

Let me add two things. One is that you can find a person and, as Bonnie said, you could stop there. But it always happened that when we would come across, say, maybe a name we heard once upon a time but never thought about, we found an entire universe attached to their networks. So that's one way of discovering what has been erased because there's always something attached, there's always something there that involves many more people and many more ideas than come to the surface. I also want to respond to you as the editor of a journal [*Journal of Sociolinguistics*] which, you know, is often held up as being one of the most important journals and I could take this as a challenge, right?

How to do this better? How to be attentive to every last detail of the practice of what we do? Who I want to invite as associate editors or who do I think I am to accept an invitation, right? Who can I work with? Who do you invite as reviewers? What do you do with the reviews? We've just started an initiative called *Decentering the Anglosphere*. How do we do this in really concrete, practical terms? Because if we can't do it in our everyday practice, I don't know where we're going to go. I've been talking to Miguel Pérez Milans, who's one of the co-editors of the journal *Language Policy*. We're trying to develop a conversation around this and there are lots of us. We understand this as an issue and we have to find the ways of practicing. I feel like we're trying to help each other. I'll take all the help I can from you to figure out how to do things differently.

## Busi Makoni

Just a small comment on that. I think, from experience, what becomes a challenge by not letting Black women into scholarship is: How can we then challenge some of the theoretical frameworks that exist that do not address issues that are pertinent to our own local communities, if we do not have the space to do so?

## Heller

Right, and speaking from my position, a position of, you know, reasonable amount of power as editor of a journal, how do I help those spaces happen?

## Atila Calvente (Federal University of Rio de Janeiro, Brazil)

So nice to be here. Thank you very much. The book has inspired me to remember that the World Bank made some interventions in the Amazon in the 1970s and in the 1980s on small farms, a kind of land reform is what the military government would say. I saw the Paiter Suruí people have problems with the kind of intervention from the World Bank. The money from the World Bank was for the big companies to build a road, which caused many other problems in the Amazon: destruction of the forest, the fauna and flora, etc. So, after those years I started doing my PhD [in economics], now after my master degree in the 1980s in Brasilia and now I'm trying to put together those ideas, the rationalist positivist idea that economics shows us. I learned so much with your book, in terms of rhizome you connect ideas, culture, language, education and we do need a transdisciplinary approach to better understand and connect people. So, I'm working with children attending public schools here in Petrópolis, Brazil. After reading the book, I'll have to pay attention to the way I speak, the things I do with the students in the communities. Most of them in vulnerable situations, a few on the road to conflict with the law. So, I would like you to comment a little more about the idea of the rhizome, interdisciplinary, transdisciplinary and the language, the way you can motivate people to look for some kind of different education that's not just top-down. So that people can build together and get motivation to understand the historical process they're living in. You brought history to my soul, you brought so many interesting things. So, could you comment on the difficulties, the problems and mainly the possibilities when you work with people and students to make language something more than a mode of education, but something you could share with them, listen to the way they understand reality. I don't know if I express myself well.

## McElhinny

You expressed yourself eloquently, there's a lot in that question. There's a set of questions about land reform. There's a set of questions about metaphors we use, trees or rhizomes, for understanding language. And there's a question about what does anti-oppressive education look like. Those three questions are actually at the center of my work and it actually loops back around to the question we didn't answer that Makoni asked about language and land, so thank you because it gives us a chance to go a little bit further.

I'm going to give a little bit of context through my recent work and link it back to these responses. Rafael mentioned that I'm now working on water and you might be saying to yourself 'What does this work on language, capitalism and colonialism have to do with decolonial approaches to water?' There are a number of reasons why I'm thinking about water. One is, you know, in the final chapter of the book, we focus on a number of ways in which things are commodified, including language. I wanted to think about sites where people are imagining a Commons rather than a commodity. Water is a site that people more readily imagine as a Commons, than sometimes land, although the work that you do in water absolutely ends up shaping what happens on land. Water can be commodified too.

Nestlé, the international company, extracts water from aquifers in southern Ontario and pays 1/100 to a penny and then sells the bottles worldwide, so you can commodify water, it can be privatized. But water is something that is critical for people's life and people resist understanding it as a commodity. There's been very successful fight back, push back against privatization of water in a range of sites. So, water is also absolutely a characteristic of this place. One of the things I'm trying to think about, is what is the work that's shaped by the land and water of this place. 20% of the world's fresh water is in the Great Lakes. So, this is a place that has lakes and rivers everywhere. It shapes the way we imagine our everyday lives.

I wanted to think about a place-based approach. It doesn't mean it's narrowly constrained, right? Some of the fish that are in the Great Lakes migrate from the Caribbean, so there are complex connections and conversations that are being created. I wanted to think about water and I wanted to think about the kinds of alliances – and I won't say unlikely, because that's a pessimistic approach to social change, but I will say unprecedented – that have emerged in this site for thinking about how we work around water. And there are a number of unprecedented alliances linking labor and Indigenous groups, linking people who are thinking about food security and food sovereignty from Black communities, Indigenous communities, and other food insecure communities. There are multi-faith alliances thinking about the sacredness of water and… the Indigenous elders here note that in order to understand this place, people need to understand the Anishinaabek language because many of its place names encode stories, theories and relationships with water.

So, for me, one strategy is thinking, if we identify a problem of commodification, identifying another site, understanding the Commons in Indigenous territory and thinking about the work that's happening there, and what it is doing as a pushback against, but creating also alternatives. And that work on water are forms of reform. They are reimagining how food systems work and how water works in ways that I think are revolutionary.

We've used a number of natural metaphors for thinking about language. One is the family tree and [Edward] Said talks about the way in which that notion of a family tree comes about at a certain moment of colonial understanding of language and that there are challenges to that. The work that happens on pidgins and creoles is a critical and central challenge to thinking about family in particular ways and to thinking about relationship in particular ways. And the rhizome is another strategy for challenging those more tree-like metaphors. But the rhizome is still a metaphor; it's still a terrain on which we are imagining human life. So, one of the questions might be: what happens if plants, animals, land and water are not the terrain on which we're imagining what it means to be human, but are placed fully in the conversation. And for Indigenous people on these territories on which I work – Haudenosaunee, Anishinaabe – the water is kin, the plants are kin. Each of these things also speaks in its own way. So, when we think about language, the focus on language is very human centric. Even the more progressive understandings of language center it as what makes us distinctively human, what separates humans from other things. So, what might it mean to imagine those other forms of communication? How those things speak? How do we make sure we're not speaking for them? You know all of those lead us towards… lead me towards because some of you might already be there. I'm just catching up, asking how we think about communities in particular places; the ways in which they are shaped by those places; the ways in which we responsibly build interactions with each other and with the land and water of the place.

Regarding the question of an anti-oppressive education, I would say this week I'm feeling somewhat pessimistic because I think many of the institutions that we're in are not meant to build forms of solidarity and care. Large research-based institutions, like the one Monica and I are in, are often set up to sort out and to create hierarchies with marking systems, with the merit pay schemes that are used, with student competition for space and resources. And so, we have to work within those and I'm looking for the sites within the institution that are working actively against that sorting and creating relationships of solidarity and care. There's an enormous apparatus in place. For me, the moments that are most inspiring are the moments when I'm able to take students right outside of that classroom that exists in the university and I imagine other forms of classrooms and build conversations with communities. I'll offer one example.

Canada celebrates itself as a site of multiculturalism in ways that obscure colonial and racist practices. A few years ago, with a group of students, we did a solidarity trip to the University of Hawai'i at Mānoa where they have a community-engagement program. Students in that program spend time throughout the year doing work on the land and in community, in thoughtfully supervised ways that are shaped by community members. We joined some of the activities. One of them was a circle of people in a working-class community who had fought back against a gated community. There is a gated community that was being built for people who can afford to live in gated communities in Hawai'i, so wealthy middle-class, upper middle-class, people can live high up in the mountains. There was a place where people grew things. There was and is a community garden. And they successfully fought back against the gated community. They fought back against the gated community. They got a 100-year lease to build community gardens. They hired a few people to maintain the gardens, but then members of the community could participate in those gardens, once a week or once a month. And if they did, on the day that they participated, they helped tend gardens, they learned to tend the gardens, they gained those skills. At the end of each work day, there was a feast where people met, worked and talked together and they each took away a box of food from the farm. And the food from that farm also supported a café in the local hospital. That hospital is trying to think about how to care for bodies, minds and souls that were dealing with the physical, mental and spiritual trauma of being in a capitalist, in colonial society. So there was a holistic sense of health there. The work that inspires me here is work where people are doing some of the same kinds of things. They're fighting back against the gated communities and that can be a metaphor for sites of exclusion. But also creating circles of solidarity and care, maybe trying to find some strategies that don't rely on global supply chains or problematic labor practices to produce food in everyday life, and trying to imagine health differently.

Those are the places where I'm trying to invest my work and there are comparable organizations. Sometimes you hear of an example somewhere else, or you encounter it and then you come back home and say 'OK, what's happening here?' So, there are organizations doing some of that same work on building community gardens on public land, on building solidarities between communities. Right now, especially, a lot of people are concerned about food. Part of the reaction to Covid was we were concerned about the interruption of global food chains. As well as in Canada, elderly people in long-term care homes being a site where there are large numbers of Covid cases and deaths. So, too, are some of the food processing sites, the meat processing plants, and agricultural workers because they've been housed in barracks on site. So, we're diagnosing a range of ways in which food and work needs to be rethought. That's the response to questions of thinking about land reform and rhizomes. Rhizomes become quite literal in this model. People are growing things in an anti-oppressive education.

## Heller

Let me just add two quick things. One is that what I learned from the book is how much work it took to extract language from the rest of social life and so part of what I think we're talking about is reimagining: 'Well, so, what if we didn't? What if language weren't extracted?' That's institutionally a challenge because most of us have our credentials and our jobs based on some kind of expertise in something called 'language'. But that was something that got concocted and can get *un*concocted.

The other quick comment is that any metaphor we use, any way in which we talk about things, has consequences, so it has affordances. Thinking about things as trees, descendants and kinship, indeed, allows certain kinds of things and it cuts off other kinds of possibilities.

Both Bonnie and I are interested in looking at things in ways that are more interconnected, but that allow for an understanding of the complex, often hard to predict, sometimes perverse consequences of the ways in which things work together. I think that it's part of my job to try to understand them, but that then requires me to think about things as not structured in a top-down way and not requiring particular units of things which are homogeneous and bounded off from each other.

## Shaila Sultana (University of Dhaka, Bangladesh)

Hi, this is Shaila from the University of Dhaka, Bangladesh. I have really enjoyed reading your book in the sense that you mentioned positionality, multiplicity and awareness and, in fact, you have positioned yourself very clearly. And the way you have built your own stories into the writing, I have totally enjoyed it. I know that you have this specific focus on language, colonization and capitalism, but somehow you have managed to keep a very comprehensive, holistic understanding of how this field has evolved over the years. So, I think it will be a very good reference book for years to come. And I really didn't know about the stories behind all the research done by these scholars, for example, Gramsci, Labov and Gumperz. I have read about them. But I haven't read about their interesting backgrounds and inspirations to come into this specific field before. For example, Gumperz came to the Indian subcontinent in 1947 and he worked for the language policy. Even though I'm located in Bangladesh, this specific information is quite new for me. I would also like to say that your last sentence is quite compelling 'Walking backward into future'. When I think of walking backward to future from my context, I see that my backward is leading to colonialism itself. For more than 300 years, the ideas of colonialism have influenced our concept of language or concept of language policies and practices. For example, I can mention a specific research study that I'm doing at the moment. We have a very small number of Indigenous communities. The primary school classes are taken in Bangla, the national language. So, in this classroom and in the university the Indigenous languages are totally absent. They are not used at all. Even in informal domains, for example, families, the use of Indigenous languages has become less and less present because of the governmental policies, and immense importance given to Bangla and English.

Now, when I talk to the teachers in this context, they are not ready to do anything at all for saving their languages because they themselves see the commodification of language as more pertinent to their life. That's why the communities themselves want to learn Bangla; the communities themselves want to learn English. They are not at all interested to preserve their language. So, in these situations, people like us, the researchers like us, what will we do? What should be our way for decolonizing ourselves, who are very much aware of all the theories that have been introduced by the European applied linguists? At the same time, when people here in the community are very much influenced by ideologies, they're more into the materialistic achievements that they may gain through languages. So, in what ways can we decolonize our own selves and our practices?

### Heller

So, for me, the issue is not one purely of ideology, but it is material in the sense that there are reasons why people do what they do. I think our job is to understand and take really seriously why it is that people value what they value. Usually, it's a really reasonable understanding of what (to use Bourdieu's term) the linguistic market is like and what one's position is within that, what kind of access to resources you do or do not have, and how you can get what you need to get in order to survive and prosper. So I don't think it's a matter so much of decolonizing minds as it is of understanding what the nature is of the systems in which we're located, in which the value attributed to language, main languages or linguistic varieties, or whatever we want to call them, how those are bound up with the possibility of participating in spaces where important symbolic and material resources are produced, where their value is attributed, where their circulation is controlled. So, the real question is: what is the material source of the value that's attributed to linguistic resources? And: what opportunities do people have to position themselves with respect to that? Within that I think it is really important – Bonnie mentioned this earlier – to think about what it is that educational institutions do. We are taught to think of them as avenues of social mobility, avenues of opportunity.

But, as agencies of the state, they're also about making the right kind of citizen, disciplining bodies and minds, and doing social selection (as Bourdieu and Passeron and the new sociology of education in the 1960s and 1970s pointed out). There's a lot of existing work about the sorting mechanism and the discursive masking of the social selection processes that in many respects educational institutions are for. I think we do have a problem of a disconnect between what we would like to believe about educational institutions, what we would like them to do, and what they actually do. So, the work, maybe, lies there more than it lies in convincing people that their linguistic varieties or languages have more value than they think they do.

## Sultana

But the system itself is so much ideologically laden that it becomes problematic to find a way to convince the stakeholders, the government, and the education system. At the same time, the people who are at the grassroots level are not as well ready to mobilize themselves in order to raise their voices. So, we are sort of stranded in the middle trying to figure out in what ways we can address these issues. On the one hand, we have governmental and educational institutions, which have certain ideologies. On the other hand, we have the people who are in the system at the grassroots level. They are also influenced by ideologies. Perhaps if they could have raised their voices, some way or another, they could have made themselves visible to the government. But we can't make any of these parties work the way you know the thing should be.

## Heller

Marilyn Martin-Jones and I talked about this a long time ago in an introduction to a volume we edited called *Voices of Authority* (2001); we put it in terms of interstices. There are different ways in which you can accomplish institutional change, right? And the challenge is what's possible to do from within and what is not. But there's always spaces where things are not locked down, the spaces of contradiction. And you put your finger on this huge contradiction for states legitimized through ideologies of democracy, which failed to deliver on the promise. So, where do these contradictions show up in people's lives? Where do they show up in institutional practice? Those are the points where you can start making spaces to say ok, how do we think about this contradiction? How do we work with that? That's not a revolutionary concept. It's not a revolutionary practice. But it's one that can have material consequences maybe, most importantly, locally and more broadly, as things go on. But there are always those spaces.

The image that always comes to mind is from the work of a former student of mine, Alessandra Renzi, who is now at Concordia University in Montreal and was part of the squatter movement in Naples at the time when Berlusconi owned the entire apparatus of the Italian media. There was no possibility for using the media to develop any other kind of narrative than the one that Berlusconi had. But they discovered that the cones of broadcast signals would overlap in ways which, at a neighborhood level, allowed you to tap into the broadcast signal, and do what they called pirate TV. And so they would set up neighborhood-level TV stations where people from the neighborhood could come in, tap into Berlusconi's system and tell their stories. People could come and yell at their neighbors for not dealing with their garbage properly, in a different conversational space, a different mediatized space from the state-level one. So that's a material example of what I'm talking about.

## McElhinny

Well, I think in many ways we keep looping back to Sinfree Makoni's questions. He had asked a question that I think we didn't answer at all and that was a question about which ideas of language are liberatory, or that might look liberatory and are not.

There are so many moments when people think they have an idea of what progress is going to be and they create structures to impose that idea of progress on others. In Canada, one of those examples is residential schools where Indigenous children were taken from their parents and placed in educational institutions that were seen as preparing them for the future that the state thought was the right future for them. Part of that practice was the erasure of Indigenous languages. People were punished for using languages. There were sites of a range of forms of violence. This is where Monica's cautions about hope are ones I take on board because there are hopes that are racist and there are hopes that are sexist and there are hopes that are violent. There was a hope embodied in that project. It was a problematic form of hope. It was the eradication of Indigenous ways of being, including Indigenous languages.

There are a lot of moments where I'm wary of benevolence, including my own, right? So, I think we need to rethink ideas of progress, but we can't do it for other people. People will imagine for themselves what that progress needs to be. What we can do as educators is not imagining what progress is. I think it is helping to support people in becoming competent resistors. And then they can resist as they see fit. There's a toolkit that you need to create a competent resistor. You need to be able to diagnose institutions. You need a set of histories. You need a set of social media tools these days. You need a set of writing tools. So, we can help people become competent resistors and they can ask the questions and move the work forward.

I do think what our work is requiring us to do is reimagine time, reimagine space and reimagine what it means to be a person. All of those things are happening in our work.

And part of reimagining time is asking what we imagine progress to be. Reflecting not just on other people's notions of progress, but on our own. What is it that we imagine it to be and how is that shaping our work?

I think the question of place is something I spoke to earlier. What does that mean for us not to be disembodied, as in some ways we are in this conversation, but what does it mean to be fully anchored in the place where we are? And think about the questions that emerge from that place, its histories, but also the land, the water, the plants and the animals that are there. They shape the life of all of that. The rivers that run in Toronto, the lakes, the rivers that were buried as the city was being built, all shape the life of this city.

What do we imagine a good person is? I have been in plenty of circles – and I imagine you have been too – progressive sites where I felt like people were not embodying the future that I wanted us to be working in. There are moments when I have to work on what it means to work collectively, because I have been educated in a competitive system. So, what does it mean to work collectively? What does it mean to work with kindness and care?

## Heller

In that sense, I think it's a matter not just of trying to work towards competent resistance but also competent wielding of power.

## Editors' note

*At this point of the conversation, one participant made an intervention about the role of one's locus of enunciation in the production and circulation of academic knowledge. The responses from Monica and Bonnie follow:*[1]

## Heller

I think there are lots of ways in which we tried to write in exactly that way. There are limits to our abilities to do that; it's a lot easier to account for somebody else's trajectory than it is to account for one's own. So that's, you know, the reflexive turn in some ways. The issue still remains, though, of what counts as a legitimate account and who gets to decide what makes sense, what's convincing, what's persuasive. But that opens it up as a matter of struggle, at least.

## McElhinny

I think because we're linguists, you know, it's thinking about what does a statement do. Here in Canada – and I would welcome hearing what the discussion is from each of the sites where you're at – many institutions are issuing statements of solidarity this week. Statements that are critical of policing violence, that are critical of anti-Black racism, and there's a profound discussion about that. There are companies that have never done the work that are issuing these statements. The University of Toronto's president issued a statement. I drafted a statement for the college and sent it out for review. And I was rightly critiqued for doing it too quickly, without more and more meaningful consultation, but most importantly for writing a statement of solidarity rather than a statement of accountability. There's a series of conversations about (i) how we need to go beyond the debate to say the statement does not perform the action that it describes as needed, (ii) who has the right to speak about what needs to be done, and (iii) in what ways are statements the performance of a form of virtue – and I would say in this context of performance of White virtue that doesn't actually push us into making the institutional transformations that are required. So, what I want us to think about is: in what ways does our work move beyond being a statement about what needs to be done, a description about what needs to be done, a form of solidarity expression? When and how does that work engage in the practice of institutional transformation, engaged in doing the work that we're describing?

Universities are a critical site for that work. When I look at the college that I'm in, although it houses programs as I mentioned in African studies, Equity studies and Caribbean studies, it supports student organizations, there's been very little work done over the past 40 years in proactively recruiting Black staff in the student-service facing positions. There's work to do. There's always work to do. We need to think about the very real power we wield in the institutions that we're in to undertake transformations and think about the exclusions, inclusions in an ongoing work. That's accountability as well.

### Lomeu Gomes

OK, well unfortunately we're reaching the end of this very stimulating discussion, and I'd like to thank once again Bonnie and Monica for so kindly accepting this invitation to join us today. And of course, all of you who attended and asked questions and commented on the chat because you made the discussion happen and I'm really glad to see this happening. It started off almost two years ago with Alistair Pennycook, Sinfree Makoni, Lynn Mario and perhaps one or two more people trying to discuss *On Decoloniality*, by Mignolo and Walsh (2018). So from four to five participants to 55 or 60 today, it's really, really nice. So, thank you so much. Makoni, would you like to make some final comments?

### Makoni

I would like to thank everybody for participating. It has been wonderful to have a chance of listening and engaging with you. Thank you very much.

### Heller

Thank you very much for allowing us to join this incredible group and unbelievable conversation. It's quite a privilege.

### McElhinny

Rafael and Makoni thank you very much. I welcome the opportunity to hear more about the work of this group. This is an amazing forum that the two of you have convened, an amazing lineup. The point of this is at getting an opportunity to hear more about work that other people are doing, so I'm putting my email up in the chat.

I would welcome hearing from you in email or if your work is in a place where you're prepared to share it, I would love to create further conversation. Thank you so much.

## Note

(1)   The editors were unable to reach the participant to obtain their consent to reproduce their intervention in full.

## References

Connell, R. (2007) *Southern Theory: The Global Dynamics of Knowledge in Social Science.* Cambridge and Malden, MA: Polity Press.

Heller, M. and Martin-Jones, M. (eds) (2001) *Voices of Authority: Education and Linguistic Difference.* Westport, CT: Ablex.

Heller, M. and McElhinny, B. (2017) *Language, Capitalism, Colonialism: Toward a Critical History.* Toronto: University of Toronto Press.

Klein, N. (2017) *No is Not Enough: Resisting Trump's Shock Politics and Winning the World We Need.* Chicago, IL: Haymarket Books.

Mignolo, W.D. and Walsh C.E. (2018) *On Decoloniality: Concepts, Analytics, Praxis.* Durham, NC: Duke University Press.

Pennycook, A. and Makoni, S. (2019) *Innovations and Challenges to Applied Linguistics from the Global South.* Abingdon and New York: Routledge.

# 4  Black Bodies

Robbie Shilliam

### Rafael Lomeu Gomes

Robbie Shilliam is Professor of International Relations in the Department of Political Science at Johns Hopkins University. Professor Shilliam researches the political and intellectual complicities of colonialism and race in the global order. He is co-editor of the Rowman & Littlefield book series, Kilombo: International Relations and Colonial Questions. Robbie was a co-founder of the Colonial/Postcolonial/Decolonial working group of the British International Studies Association and is a long-standing active member of the Global Development section of the International Studies Association. Currently, Robbie is working on three strands of inquiry: firstly, a re-reading of classical political economy through its intimate relationship to Atlantic slavery, with a bearing towards contemporary controversies regarding 'social conservatism'; secondly, a retrieval of Ethiopianism as a critical orientation towards global order, especially in terms of its cultivation of a tradition of anti-colonial anti-fascism from the 1930s onwards; and thirdly, South-South anti-colonial connections, especially between peoples of the African Diaspora and Indigenous movements. His book *Decolonizing Politics* was published by Polity Press in 2021.

Welcome, once again Robbie, and thank you for accepting our invitation.

### Sinfree Makoni

Before our speaker for today takes the floor, we need to welcome two other guests. It gives me great pleasure to introduce Professor Cheryl Sterling, who is the director of African Studies here at Penn State. We're thankful for the support that the program is giving us in this African Studies Global Virtual Forum. So, we thought that formally it would be good to invite Cheryl so that she can be able to situate for us the Global Forum within the vision of African Studies at Penn State. Welcome Professor Sterling.

### Cheryl Sterling (Pennsylvania State University, USA)

Thank you for inviting me. We can easily say that we're kind of living in the aftermath of the colonial encounter for the most part, or it's maybe a colonially defined world. Whether we say that we agree with the supposition that colonialism and the racial categorization that we've inherited come from economic drivers or these racial suppositions led to domination and economic opportunities, it still brings us to this moment of protests that we see happening,[1] protests and demands for change in our understandings of the paradigms of westerneity.

My particular area is Blackness and Black subjectivity, which I call a 'denigatory Blackness'. This kind of racialism or racism, which leads to many of our stereotypes and also spawns and again, a sense of transcendent Whiteness, has created, of course, collective issues that we are all grappling with, to a certain extent. Albert Memmi so aptly named and operationalized the term a 'pyramid of tyrannies' about previously dominated groups. Well, he was talking about dominated groups and racism. But we can apply this now to previously dominated groups as each are vying to reach the top of this very pyramid, the apex of the power scheme. So, what does this mean for us? In these systems of domination across the board, whether racialized or not, we realize it's all about power. Who has the power to control everything, to control life, to control death, to control resources, to control all levels of currency, but within this epoch we're seeing, or moment in time, we're seeing a mobilized youth force, in a very short period of time, who are wrestling with these monumental aspects of control. As Dr Makoni has asked me specifically to address African Studies here, what we find in academia are the more institutionalized aspects of control of knowledge and resources. And, more specifically in Penn State, with our program, as our goal is to grow our faculty and to strengthen our base and offer curriculum that more structurally integrates the continent in ways that benefit our students, this institutionalized top-down model of knowledge production resists transformation for a program such as ours.

And what we see in our area, what's called 'Happy Valley', the youth have not caught up with the rest of the world to demand or call for change in the institutional order that would shift this type of distribution of knowledge. And while they [the youth] address the larger macro structures attached to the globality of struggle over Black lives, we have a lot of work to do to connect that struggle to the parallelisms of Euro-dominance or colonial domination in the collective discourse and in our inheritance. I read in one of the articles from Dr Shilliam about collective inheritance of inferiority, meniality and unintelligence. And so, this is where I'd like to just leave us and bring us all into the discussion.

## Makoni

Thank you very much, Professor Sterling. You raised quite a number of important issues which I think Robbie Shilliam will address as we go along, issues about protests, student engagement in protests and issues about Whiteness or Blackness in the academia. Before we go to the conversation, I'd like to also welcome Unyierie Idem who is a professor of English as a second language. She has a PhD in Applied Linguistics and is a poet. She's going to be reading one of her poems called 'Black Bodies'.

## Unyierie Idem (Holyoke Community College, USA)

Good morning, good afternoon, everyone. Thank you so much for this opportunity. When Sinfree Makoni approached me to read a poem during a session like this, I was kind of surprised and wondered what poetry would really contribute to the discussion. But I didn't want to disappoint him [laughing] so I agreed. And I thought I would read something out of an already existing collection that I have. I toyed around with a couple of poems, but then I decided that will be too general. And I would write something new and sort of more specific to the topic that we're going to discuss today. So, the title of this poem, which by the way is still a work in progress, is 'Black Bodies'.

They traverse the halls of learning, dressed
in the fine livery of diversity – this meandering
of Black bodies juxtaposed in public spaces
once deemed a distant speculation.

They exude an array of talents and values,
a coalition of experiences, to break the
monotony of homogeny.

Yet, between the segregated enclaves of the past
and the lofty citadels of future aspirations,
stands the stark reality of the present.

Of the veiled truth behind the warm
speeches and friendly gestures,

of the bitter reminders of their mandated
status by legal decrees and amendments,
without which 'they would have no presence',

of the constant questioning of their expertise
and scholarship, of the unattainable
parity dictated by the status quo,

of the subtle microaggressions and the
dehumanizing stereotypes that make them
the tokenized pieces on the board game –
ornate and strategically placed for optimum
exploitation of their invisible labor.

They are the pawns of social marginalization
and bureaucratic politicization.
They are the objectified targets of secret
glances through half closed doors.
They are the subjects of quiet whispers
in the dark alleys of power.

Nonetheless, this massive wave of dark bodies,
invincible in its pursuit, ebbs and flows to
defy the current. As the wind of change blows
in new directions, the swollen tributaries
of epistemic quest cascade into global waters.

This journey begun in the ages is far from
over until Black bodies find their pedestal.

## Makoni

Thank you very much, Unyierie. It looks like a number of things are beginning
to come together. A number of issues are beginning to get foregrounded. One of
these things which is being foregrounded is what Robbie Shilliam refers to as Black
cognitive incompetence. Robbie, can I begin by asking you what exactly did you
mean by Black cognitive incompetence in your article ['Behind the Rhodes statue'].

## Robbie Shilliam

Thanks, it's really great to be here with everybody. I'm excited about the conversation and where it's going to go. I've got no idea [laughing].

The cognitive competency is probably a bit more of a contemporary term for
something which I think probably underwrites a lot of the colonial racial order. That
is about an ability to reason which is adequate for the present, but beneath that,
actually, which is virtuous, and so we can think about that in terms of the founding
debates in race in the 1400s about conversion of Jews and Muslims to Christianity,
and then in the 16th century Americas about whether the 'Indios' were competent
enough to understand that Jesus Christ was their Lord and Savior. We know the kind
of histories of the continent, the way in which conquest comes with conversion. Even
in Las Casas you find this thing: Are these non-Latin Christians able to reason?

The basic argument is about a religious competency for virtuous action, which
then shifts in a lot of ways. One shift we can think about is the late 18th century
when that competency becomes linked to the ability to improve one's environment.
And that's very much linked with all the Scottish philosophers, classical political
economy, Adam Smith, Adam Ferguson, all these guys – and it becomes more of a
profane metric about a competency to be human. So very much in the Sylvia Wynter
vein: Reason, Rationality and Humanity are interlinked and adjudicated consistently
and that's one of the underlying things with colonialism, and then by the time we get
to 20th-century anthropologists like Bronislaw Malinowski, this is all about development. Do people have a cognitive competency, by which they can undertake and
experience change in an orderly and civil fashion, or is the only way that they can
deal with colonial development in terms of disorder and revolt?

## Makoni

Okay, I understand your argument. In the preface to your book, *The Black
Pacific* (Shilliam, 2015), Bhambra raises the following point. She says: what would
theory look like if it was going to be created and written by individuals who are not
normally expected to be theorizing. My question to you, then is: What does theory
look like for you if you're writing from a different perspective, different from dominant theory-formation?

### Shilliam

Oh, what a question [laughing]. I'm not sure what it looks like! I sometimes try to play with this thing about 'living knowledge traditions'. Or, let me put it like this. There is an attenuation of what counts as theory – especially political or social theory – whereby theory becomes an author. And even Foucault becomes an author and Foucauldians treat Foucault as author, right? So, it becomes individualized, it becomes written, and it also becomes written in a format which is notably theoretical, i.e. as an abstracted vocabulary. Along with that, theory then becomes not so much about doing but simply about thinking. That to me is the place that we could start to rethink theory. So, one of my favorite examples is Amy Ashwood Garvey, Marcus Garvey's first wife who was an incredibly consequential figure in Pan African thought in the 20th century. At a pivotal moment, the Pan-African Congress in Manchester in 1945, she is the only person who raises gender issues at the conference. She is perhaps more responsible than Marcus Garvey for recruiting people to the Universal Negro Improvement Association (UNIA), on the streets of Harlem, and elsewhere. Unlike Marcus she's actually a Pan-African and there's a slight distinction one can make between being a Black nationalist and a Pan-African. She travels the world. She has all these designs on writing books, she talks about race, color, class, gender, propriety. She promises to write all these books. In the end, the only thing written of any consequence, and which is publicly available, is her autobiographical note about how she started the UNIA.

Amy Ashwood Garvey wants to write about women in West Africa, but never publishes these writings. If one were to just dwell with these literary 'failings', then Amy Ashwood Garvey could never be a theorist. And yet her theory was practice. How was it that she was able to communicate with and persuade a whole sway of different peoples, Black peoples of different nationalities, different classes, different locations to come and join the UNIA? The International African Service Bureau, which was the famous body comprised of George Padmore, C.L.R. James, Chris Braithwaite etc., was a vanguard of the intellectual struggle against Italian Fascism in the 1930s. But they formed in Amy Ashwood Garvey's parlor, which was in the Florence Mills nightclub in London. So, was Amy just a cook? Or did her organizational-intellectual work actually help to direct some key Pan-African practices and traditions of thought? Now, political theory couldn't say much about Amy Ashwood Garvey directly because there's not a text. Her praxis is not written in the abstract register. So how many more Amy Ashwood Garveys are there?

### Makoni

You talk about decolonization. What does decolonization mean both in theory and in practice to you? And how is it distinct from other forms of anti-racist initiatives in institutions such as universities? Why did it gain traction in universities? What does it mean to apply a template which emerged from a specific historical, political and geographical context to another context? For example, what is the difference between decolonization and diversity and inclusion?

To sum up: What is the relationship between theory and practice in decolonization institutionally? What is the nature of the relationship between decolonization and discourses of diversity and inclusion?

## Shilliam

I think the first thing to talk about is the way in which the university, especially from the mid- to the late 1800s onwards, becomes the site wherein the liberal arts affirms that the whole society will benefit from your mind, if not the world. There's a certain claim about doing liberal arts which corresponds to the classical idea of cultivating the mind to serve humanity.

At the same time, the university is an incredibly segregationist institution. Just think about the debate between W.E.B. DuBois and Booker T. Washington. The debate is fundamentally about the place Black people should have in higher education. Should it be a technical place – a technical vocation – or should it be a liberal place – the edification of the mind and the furtherance of humanity? What's very interesting is that a lot of Black students want to come and learn the classics, i.e. the Greeks and the Romans. Why? Is it because they have drunk the Kool-Aid and they think that the only legitimate form of human civilization has been the Greeks and Romans? Maybe a few do, but I don't think that's really in their mind. Rather, they are thinking this: if we are to be treated as fully human, and if to be fully human is to be able to competently reason about the world in generally consequential terms, then we have to prove that we can do the classics. We have to prove that we can do the Greeks and the Romans.

The university then takes on a particular function of a colonial rule. And it's a settler colonial rule which distinguishes who are the reasonable and non-reasonable groups, meaning: who is able to think about their own situation and others in a competent fashion, and who can only ever be thought about. And that distinction then leads to the prospect of 'decolonizing' academia.

If you think about the tradition of thought which has come to us in various ways through Black Lives Matter, you can start to think about the stakes that are playing in this. Communities which are policed can only ever be thought about and liberals can only ever say they feel bad about them. But what if those communities have traditions of thought which are not only illuminating their own situation but illuminating the broader structures which everybody falls under? That means that we have to think about decolonizing the academy, so to speak, as one element in a broader reparation of power as Professor Sterling said at the beginning. This is about power.

## Makoni

How do discourses about diversity and inclusion fit in there?

## Shilliam

There's a couple of ways. In the intra-academic work that I've done, I've rarely led it with a language of social justice. I've always led it with an institutional language of pedagogy and competency because many academics and managers presume that a focus on social justice partializes the pursuit of knowledge. On the one hand, that language can be used instrumentally to do certain things. On the other hand, at the same time, it's a language of deferral and of inclusion. In colonial times there was a 'native' intelligentsia; today, there's a sense of bringing people in to disarm them. And anything which breaks from that is seen as a disorderly and irrational project. I think that links in some ways to Unyierie's poem at the beginning, this sense about walking through architecture, but not ever having been able to change the architecture.

## Makoni

Okay, good. Thank you very much for an exciting conversation.

## Lomeu Gomes

That was a great initial conversation. Perhaps I could start with a question which relates to a point that you made, Robbie, before we started the discussion itself about the differences between academia in the UK and the US. And I'd like to ask if you could bring back that discussion by establishing a parallel with a point that you make towards the end of your article when you talk about the importance of not having this 'ideal' concept of an academia. Or rather how it would be useful to actually engage with empire's academic legacies and the dispositions that you present (i.e. colonial development, race relations, and the cognitive competency of familiar strangers) in your article.

## Shilliam

Well, let me start by saying that I think an actual Global History of the colonial heritage of higher educational universities is yet to be fully written. I wouldn't be able to make any kind of synthetic argument. But at the least, we could say that all these people are talking to each other. When Oxford, in 1807, puts out a famous defense of liberal education against the instrumentalization of the university, then Yale does the same thing about two decades later, and both defend ownership of the university for a particular 'caste'. And then of course Whiteness doesn't become phenotypical in the straightforward biological way, it becomes a kind of a mode of thought and action oriented towards exclusion and segregation.

That being said, there are distinct differences. For example, a lot of the post-colonial literature in the Anglo Academy initially came from the Commonwealth. Why the Commonwealth? Because in the UK there is this very entrenched idea that all the bad shit, pardon my French, happened in the colonies, but never in England. It could never have happened there. It was always these people who went out to the colonies and became twisted by the climate into irrational despots. So, there is this preservation of a pure, unblemished heart of civilization, even in the midst of Empire, which is very much what underwrites the disposition of a lot of the English cultural class. So, in other words, there is consistent hiving off of all the violence and irrationality which comes with colonialism to the colonies, so that the English heart of empire is never sullied by imperialism. Then postcolonialism initially comes to Commonwealth literature because it's all right to talk about race in South Africa, it's all right to talk about race in Jamaica, but it's not all right to talk about race in England, that's rude. Right? [laughing].

Now you can compare and contrast the UK to the US. I'm not in any way wanting to claim that the US is somehow 'better'. But there is a reason why, even with all the struggles, Black Studies found a place in the US Academy and even though the same struggles took place in the UK, Black Studies did not find a place in the British Academy. There's something about the heart of empires, which is slightly different to the settler colonies in the colonies, some of which then become empires themselves, no doubt. In any case, this geography does make a slight difference in terms of our conversations about racism and the legacies of colonialism in the academy.

## Makoni

Let me just jump in and give you some figures. In the UK in 2017 there were 18,510 full professors and only 85 who were Black, and there were only 20 who were women. In Applied Linguistics since the passing away of the Nigerian professor called Tope Omoniyi, there were no full professors in Applied Linguistics who were Black in the UK.

## Shilliam

Yes, and in those terms, things are way better in the US, that's for sure. But structurally, it's very similar. If you go down to assistant professors, you've got more black, brown, more women. If you go to contingent faculty, way more. If you go onto campus and you look at who's doing the cooking and the cleaning and the security, chances are you'll see a racialized distinction between those staff and faculty. Basically, UK academia has managed to preserve its cultural purity [laughing] better than the US but that structure is very, very similar – even in terms of who gets grants, who gets the funding of certain programs. I'd be incredibly surprised if Gender Studies, Africana Studies, etc. are not going to be disproportionately hit by all the cutbacks in budgets following Covid-19.

## Bassey Antia (University of the Western Cape, South Africa)

Hi. I was just wondering if you see any commonalities between the movements in South Africa around Rhodes and Black Lives Matter, Why is my Curriculum so White, and all of that. We've seen in Oxford statues falling as well as here in the US, do you see any common threads?

## Shilliam

Hmm. Yeah, that's an awesome question. But what do you think?

## Antia

Well, I think this is interesting that all of this is coming together at about this time. So, there is a coming together, I think, of a number of forces trying to bring about change, making it possible for us to hear voices that have typically been suppressed in higher education and elsewhere. We've seen what's happening in Oxford, but I'm not quite sure of the similarities. Given your location in the US, do you see similar things happening there?

## Shilliam

I do and I don't. I think the links between the South African Rhodes Must Fall (RMF) and the UK RMF, mainly coming out of Oxford, are quite obvious primarily because there's a lot of South African people in the UK. It's that simple. A lot of South African people, a lot of African people, whether they were born there and their parents weren't, or whether they come in as young adults, it is that kind of immediacy that is very important to actually think about the organizing that people have been doing. There is an argument about the movement in South Africa, which I do not fully subscribe to but has important elements to it: there was a moment when it could have been a movement to crack open all the structural inequalities from apartheid but then it became a movement for the elite. Interestingly, in the UK, the universities which have by far the most black and brown students are not elite universities. They are almost the equivalent of community colleges in the US. But RMF happened in the elite universities, the equivalent of R1 universities. So again, that's the similarity. The big, big difference between the two is that in South Africa there is the land question, and in the UK the land question is moot, or it's an issue of urban gentrification.

We could also think about the furor over statues. When I got to Hopkins, I realized Baltimore is basically a southern city. It was the gateway of the South and as such has pronounced histories and presents of segregation. There were two statues north and south of Hopkins's Homewood campus. I don't know if they were from the 1950s or '60s. The one to the north, a dedication to the gallant women of the South, the one to the south, a dedication to confederate General Robert Lee. After the Freddie Gray uprisings, the statues were taken away but their plinths remained, almost abandoned. In my mind, that was an act of genius, intentional or not, because the scenes remain haunted. Actually, during the student struggle against the Hopkins administration over the prospect of creating an armed private campus police force, one of those plinths was repurposed as a 'Harriet Tubman' rallying point.

But what's the difference between the US situation and that of South Africa or the UK? Well, in the US a Pan-African or global intellectual tradition about Black liberation becomes attenuated into a nationalist tradition. Not all intellectuals in the US accepted that, yet it's still difficult to gain traction in US Black Studies via an anti-imperial critique. When you look at the statues, the statue debate in the rest of the world is about imperial figures, in the US it's all about the South. And I'm not saying it shouldn't be about the South, but I'm saying if you look at the South, you should not look at the South except to look at it in the global perspective. Louisiana, French Caribbean, Puerto Rico, Texas, Mexico, Philippines: they all come together in a history of imperial expansion and contestation.

## Lynn Mario de Souza (University of São Paulo, Brazil)

You may already have answered this. But let me first situate where I'm speaking from. I'm speaking from one of the elite universities in Brazil. And in spite of what you mentioned that Lula made changes demographically to education in Brazil, I would say, this happens more at an undergraduate level at universities. At postgraduate level very little changes occurred. In my university, for example, the selection process into the postgraduate courses MAs and PhDs is still done through interviews. Black Brazilian candidates tend to be at a disadvantage in face-to-face interviews. What I'm talking about is the vulnerability of those deemed ontologically invisible by power. I'm wondering here, if it's not already a lost cause to attempt to prove cognitive equality, when the problem is the denial of ontological visibility. The ontological invisibility produced by power. So, what do we have to do? Do we have to change the power structure to produce, to generate ontological visibility, or is the whole discussion going on in Brazil at the moment about racism just epistemic and not ontological?

## Shilliam

Those are really important issues and very similar actually to, I would say, the UK and even the US. Outside of particular study areas that inclusion has always been at the bottom and the structural impositions stay in place. I have a couple of friends in Brazil, who are Black/Afro Brazilians, coming in through the Lula changes in higher education funding, trying to complete PhDs, and I can see that's a struggle for them.

The question you raise is one that doesn't lie so much in the philosophical question about ontology. It lies more in a strategic question about what spaces within universities you can take over more easily. How do you link those two wider social struggles and global struggles? In what registers do you do that? Maybe I'm a pessimist but I'm a great believer that you can't talk to Caesar in the language of social justice. Don't even bother. Talk to Caesar in the language that Caesar understands and then do your thing otherwise. And there might be issues to do with that. Actually, there certainly are. But I would never have a debate about ontological Blackness with a provost [laughing]. I'm being pessimistic about it but I'm basically saying I think your question is a question of a strategy. It's not that the questions about Blackness are not important, of course they are. But once that debate has been had, then the question is a question of strategy, and the debate itself does not give you the strategy.

## de Souza

And if I may just add something: I wasn't so much referring to the philosophical, I was thinking of the strategic, but to think of the strategic is also to think of bodies.

I was thinking that when the Black body presents itself in a selection process, it's already preemptively excluded.

## Shilliam

Absolutely, which is why those people in the late 19th century wanted to be able to speak Greek. So that their voice would betray their body.

## William Dewey (Pennsylvania State University, USA)

Hello. I'm an art historian, grew up in Zimbabwe. So, I'm going to redirect things a little bit because I love that you're kind of contextualizing the history of the images that have fallen but I'm going to suggest that rather unusually the images that are falling are figurative. But there's another category of images that people have been kind of ignoring but are equally linked to Rhodes in particular, and that also kind of extends over to architecture. There is in Oxford, there is a very prominent place called Rhodes House, there are also Rhodes scholars in South Africa, there is Rhodes University and in Cape Town there is another institution Groote Schuur, which was Rhodes's residence. Especially Rhodes House and Groote Schuur, they are full of images of Great Zimbabwe birds and Rhodes acquired one and it's the only ancient bird from Great Zimbabwe, that's not been repatriated to Zimbabwe. South African government says it's a problem because it's part of heritage and so on, but basically, it's the only bird that's not been repatriated. Rhodes was obsessed with that bird and used it as a symbol of biblical Ophir because he thought Great Zimbabwe couldn't possibly have been made by Blacks etc. So, he continually used that image of the bird and it's been repeated at Oxford House. If you ever go to Oxford House, it's on the top of the dome. It's throughout the place etc., so my contention is that those are equally kind of obnoxious images and so on, rather innocuous. What do you think will happen in terms of renaming things like Rhodes University, Rhodes House, Rhodes scholars? I've written about this and I'll send you the article but my question is kind of extending beyond the physical likenesses of Rhodes, Confederate generals, etc. the naming, the naming part.

## Shilliam

Now that's really, really interesting. What do you think of this; because you've written about it?

## Dewey

Personally, I think that people don't understand that there is an obsession with these kinds of symbols. The things that people think more about are the names like Rhodes university and so on. In the United States, you know, people are now saying we need to move on and talk about naming it as well. I'm hoping that will happen, but it's just the physical likenesses.

## Shilliam

I get it. The first thing to say is that many of the people who were part of this statue movement, one of the things they wanted to do was to actually recontextualize them – either in situ, or in a museum. So instead of a plaque at Queen Mary University of London to King Leopold commemorating the glorious diplomatic encounter between Her Highness this and His Highness that, contextualize that encounter by reference to the extreme brutality that Leopold endorsed in the Congo Free State. That is a public intervention. So, I think that's the first thing. But the second consideration is whether we always need things to be named – I'm talking for example about scholarships and funds. At Hopkins we are in the process of considering whether to rename our Woodrow Wilson undergraduate fellowship program. I wonder if it needs another person's name attached to it. Do all names require a hagiography?

## Lomeu Gomes

OK, and now we have Busi who would like to ask a question about the connection between Rhodes Must Fall (RMF) in South Africa and in the UK.

## Busi Makoni (Pennsylvania State University, USA)

Okay, I'm going to ask a question actually on that. I'm just going to first add some historical background. The UK part of RMF at Oxford was initiated by the same person who initiated it in South Africa, that was Ntokozo Qwabe. The first part of it was when he went into a restaurant and bought something. And when they gave him a receipt and he was expected to give the White waitress a tip. He wrote on the receipt that we will only give a tip when Whites return the land, so connecting the issue of the land with White settlement or White presence in South Africa, which is what you say is important.

But the other side of the RMF is that the Rhodes issue started way earlier than reported. In the early 2000s the rugby team at UCT [University of Cape Town] refused to play because the Black players refused to play, saying they didn't want Rhodes to be hovering over them and looking at them while they play. They felt that the presence of the Rhodes statue was dehumanizing.

That is again the symbolic nature of statues, what they represent and the fact that even if the laws have been removed from the book, the powerful images still represent those exclusionary laws. Now what I wanted to comment on was what Lynn Mario had started with the conversation about Black bodies, that when they present themselves to evaluation processes, they are already excluded. That's 100% true but then when they are sort of led through the door to enter, they are not expected to use their traditions of thoughts. Instead, they're expected to continue the traditions of the dominant group. In fact, they are only let in so much as they are continuing that tradition, which is what makes diversity and inclusion very different. You can have a diverse group, but that doesn't necessarily mean that you have inclusion because inclusion is likely to bring about those different ways or the different traditions of thought. While we may have diversity, but with the continued dominance of Whiteness, there are also many areas in which we are closed off in many ways. Take, for instance, the issue of publication rates, the issue of who is being cited, the citation rates of Black bodies being very limited, who holds editorial positions in knowledge production reflects a particular group of individuals and it is those individuals who have a say in giving direction on what goes ahead and what doesn't. So, those different traditions of thought, those different traditions of knowledge production, those different methodologies with data sets are already closed off. With that set up, from my point of view, we will continue with talking about having diversity but whether we will ever achieve inclusion is something else. Because if we are only going to be able to achieve inclusion, if we're able to disrupt the structures that are closing us off, we can only do so if different communities are allowed to use their traditions of thought, if those ways of knowledge production are brought into the academy, are allowed into the academy. That's my only two cents. Thank you.

### Shilliam

Thank you so much for that. That's the main point I think I'm trying to make in my article. I think this is the case in the US into the 1970s, but it's probably still the case in the UK. And I would say probably it's still the case in South African universities, at least in Cape Town. Living knowledge traditions which are not those imposed by colonial rule are almost always situated on the outside or the edge of the academy.

I worked in New Zealand for five years. Every university has a Māori Studies department. Māori are the Indigenous people of New Zealand. Now, I always got the sense that to the rest of the university Māori Studies was either anthropology or maybe language training. But the people in Māori Studies considered themselves to be a mini-university. In fact, they didn't give a damn what the rest of the university thought of them. That was my sense. Their premise was that anything in the world, from molecular genomics to fertilizer to ethics, can be interrogated and usefully explained through what they call Māori knowledge systems. Every system of education has premises – even the premise of impartiality and meritocracy.

That so deeply impressed me because it wasn't a reaction to anything. It was a retrieval of something, and that retrieval was: we can do what you can do. We do it in different ways, but we can do what you can do, and we do other things too. That's the reason why most of the people in New Zealand universities could only approach Māori Studies in one or two ways – anthropology or language, just not even talk about it, or pretend it's not there.

### Lomeu Gomes

That's a very powerful and inspiring message that leads us to almost the end of our conversation. The next person up is Susan.

## Susan Coetzee-Van Rooy

I'm going to be very brief. Hello, Robbie. I'm from South Africa. I'm a sociolinguist, so I don't even want to open up the can of worms of decolonization and the language issue. Just want to say that at the North-West University where I'm proud to work in South Africa, we are working towards and exploring multilingual pedagogy. We are exploring that people use all the languages they bring to the class and to generate knowledge and to share knowledge with each other.

I just wanted to say thank you about this notion of the dual mandate if we think about decolonization. I think it's a powerful tool for us to see what are we building and what is the development agenda if there should be one. So, I just think it's a powerful tool coming from your article that can actually structure some of our thinking also in South Africa. The last thing I want to leave us with is I was really relieved as in December 2015, I don't know, those of you who follow South African politics, it was the 'fees must fall' summer and I was preparing to serve as a leader in my faculty in 2016 and I was thinking about how I serve my students and my colleagues in this atmosphere in 2016. And I was asking a colleague of mine who was also part of the struggle. And he looked at me and he basically released me, and he said: 'Look, you're a White old auntie, you will never again impact that discussion. You can trust your children, you can sit back, the youth will lead you into the future'.

And I think this intergenerational thing to me is really interesting as well and we need to respect what the younger people are bringing to the table. We have a supportive team and we must trust it. Thank you.

## Lomeu Gomes

Perhaps we have time for one final question by Juliet before we wrap it up.

## Juliet Oduor

Thank you. I'm speaking from Kenya, and I must say that Robbie's article resonated well with what I've experienced in Kenya where we have the British syllabus, which covers most of our education and yes, so then that means that, for me, there are certain issues that were raised by Robbie that I find to be applicable.

I agree that the conversation about decolonization, just as Busi said, should begin with conversations about race, equality, diversity and even increase of inclusivity in the academia. But my question is that for us to think about decolonization, what should we do first? Let's look at the lack of diverse perspectives in our syllabuses. And I'm speaking as a student. So, when I look at the syllabi that are used in my African institution, the authors of the books are from the Global North. I believe that we should first start thinking about the lack of diversity in our syllabus. Then you also acknowledge the existence of certain inequalities in academia. For example, there are certain issues that, as a woman, I'll be able to access easily certain scholarships. These are issues that I believe we must first of all tackle before we go globally and start proclaiming that we need to talk about racism, yet in our institutions, these issues still occur. Robbie, what can you say about that?

## Shilliam

Thank you, Juliet, you're raising really important points. I don't think there's much of an answer I can give which you haven't already got. But maybe one thing I can say is that you're lucky to have not just in Kenya, but in East Africa, especially in Anglo East Africa, a history of debates and struggles around exactly that question within the university setting. You've got the famous debates in Dar es Salaam college in the late 1960s to mid 1970s with Walter Rodney, Giovanni Arrighi and others about ujamaa, self-reliance, and how to decolonize an educational system that was a subordinate part of the University of London at the time.

These debates are very important and interesting to go and revisit because you'll be surprised at how contemporary they still feel. And then, of course, you guys in Kenya have got your *Decolonizing the Mind*: Ngugi wa Thiong'o's book! Interestingly, that book came partly out of a lecture series he gave at University of Auckland in New Zealand and at the time – as well as now – there was a connected debate about retaining and embedding Te Reo, the Māori language, in education.

## Makoni

Let me thank everybody for finding time to attend this session. I know that for some people it's late at night, for others it's early in the morning. It's a problem that we will continue to have in this Global Forum. We will have a series of follow-up discussions. For example, Ngugi wa Thiong'o on December 19th will be coming to talk about decolonizing African literature.

## Shilliam

I'd love to listen in on that.

## Makoni

And it's interesting how all these elements are now beginning to coalesce around the number of different things. Our last previous session focused mostly on race. It appears even in different discussions we keep returning to issues about race and power and institutional dynamics. I think Juliet's argument about institutional dynamics, students' protests and student activism is an important issue to bear in mind.

Other than that, I think I must say thank you very much, everybody.

---

**Comments from the chat box**

Shaila Sultana: And the uncivilised, uncultured, savage lazy natives! This is the attitude British imperialists had towards the colonised in the Indian Subcontinent

Susan Coetzee-Van Rooy: Again – this was fantastic dear Sinfree Makoni. THANKS for inviting us. Kind regards, Susan (NWU, SA)

SZhou: Thank you so much. Quite insightful conversation!
Cheryl Sterling: Thank you for the invitation! This was wonderful.
Tanya Charles: Important and critical discussion. Thank you!
Kimberly Rooney: Thank you for the excellent discussion! Until next time!
Atila: Thank you

## Note

(1) Black Lives Matter protests: peaceful protests all over the United States originated by the death of George Floyd on 25 May 2020 who was assassinated by police officers in Minneapolis, Minnesota. Formal protests lasted until June 11 but protesters in large US cities are expected to continue to demand an end to police brutality.

## References

Shilliam, R. (2015) *The Black Pacific: Anti-colonial Struggles and Oceanic Connections*. London: Bloomsbury.

Shilliam, R. (2019) Behind the Rhodes statue: Black competency and the imperial academy. *History of the Human Sciences* 32 (5), 3–27.

Shilliam, R. (2021) *Decolonizing Politics: An Introduction*. Cambridge and Medford, MA: Polity Press.

Wa Thiong'o, N. (1992) *Decolonising the Mind: The Politics of Language in African Literature*. East African Publishers.

# 5 Linguistics for Legal Purposes

## John Baugh

### Rafael Lomeu Gomes

John Baugh is Professor of Psychology, Anthropology, Education, English, Linguistics, and African and African-American Studies at Washington University in St. Louis and is author of the book *Linguistics in Pursuit of Justice* (Cambridge University Press, 2018). His presentation, 'Linguistics for Legal Purposes', will provide an overview of some of the ways in which linguistics can be utilized for various legal purposes. The formulation of linguistic profiling will be included, along with matters related to housing discrimination. In addition, other civil and criminal cases will be discussed, including murder cases where linguistic experimentation or survey research were essential. The presentation concludes with a critical assessment of the field of forensic linguistics.

### John Baugh

I want to thank this Forum and Professor Makoni for organizing it. I also want to acknowledge my sponsors, especially the Ford Foundation because they supported me early in my career and did so substantially throughout most of the work I have done in the US and internationally on linguistic profiling.

I meet audiences that have never encountered linguistics. I introduce them to phonetic transcription and briefly describe it as the science that tries to determine what all human languages have in common.

I'm going to be looking at six cases today where linguistic evidence was essential. The first case is not mine. It's Roger Shuy's; the others are ones that I have worked on. Roger Shuy worked on the Cullen Davis murder trial in 1978. Some of you may already be familiar with the work that he did on that case. It's the place where the field of forensic linguistics was born. Quite accidentally, Professor Shuy happened to be on a flight from Washington DC to Dallas. At the time he was a Professor of Linguistics at Georgetown University. He met a man on the flight that was an attorney working on this case.

The case was about Cullen Davis and his wife Priscilla. The case was one of attempted murder. Davis was accused of attempting to murder Priscilla and her lover. They lived in a famous mansion in Fort Worth, Texas. A famous, if not infamous, flamboyant couple with a lavish lifestyle that was envied locally and from afar.

Due to his vast wealth, Davis was able to hire a well-known criminal attorney, namely, Richard 'Racehorse' Haynes. Again, Haynes is a very famous Texas attorney and was known far and wide for his clever courtroom antics.

Of some additional significance, when Cullen Davis was arrested, he was not handcuffed; if you're an African American in the United States you are likely to know that such a practice is quite exceptional for someone who is being arrested as a murder suspect. This is a reflection of the fact that he was a multi-millionaire. It is customary procedure to handcuff someone being arrested.

This particular trial was noteworthy because the murder suspect was the wealthiest man ever to be brought to trial. He had more resources available to him than did the prosecution. He hired Roger Shuy to try to lend additional support with scientific gravity to his case. Essentially, what happened was the FBI had two recordings. They had a wiretap recording that was used by a suspect trying to get Cullen Davis to admit that he had hired him for murder, and then there was a long-distance video camera of that conversation.

When the video was revealed to the public through national news broadcasts the implication was that it was a single recording. Roger Shuy realized that the man who was on the wiretap was speaking in a normal tone of voice sitting in the car, but Cullen Davis wasn't always in the car. From time to time, Davis would get out of the car and walk around to the trunk of the car.

Professor Shuy conducted an extensive discourse analysis to show that it was quite possible that Cullen Davis was unable to hear much of what was being recorded through the wiretap. Professor Shuy then demonstrated another viable linguistic alternative, one where Mr Davis did not realize he was participating in a sting operation, which must have convinced the jury, because he was acquitted of attempted murder while simultaneously giving birth to the field of forensic linguistics.

My own work on legal matters connected with linguistics began quite by accident in fair housing. Many people who hear me speak without seeing who I am do not realize that I'm African American; they often think that I am a reasonably well-educated European American. However, I grew up in the inner city and don't always utilize the dominant dialect that is commonly described as 'Standard American English'. Like many African Americans, I often style shift depending upon my immediate speaking circumstances. Tracy Weldon has written on this topic.

Several years ago, while looking for a place to rent in the San Francisco Bay area, I realized that something was amiss when I was told by a few prospective landlords that apartments I was scheduled to examine were no longer available. I became suspicious. None of the prospective landlords explicitly stated that they were rejecting me based on my race, which they could not detect when I called to make an appointment to view the rental property. However, on a few occasions when I arrived in person, and my visual appearance confirmed that I am a Black man, I was told that the property was no longer available.

In lieu of pursuing legal relief, I decided to conduct a comparative experimental linguistic study research instead. Similar circumstances are depicted in the film, *West Side Story*. Anita tells her boyfriend, Bernardo, 'I'll get a terrace apartment'; he replies, 'Better get rid of your accent'. That scene anticipates what I have previously described as 'linguistic profiling', where a person is denied goods or services – sight unseen – during a telephone call where the service provider declines to give the prospective client what they seek because their speech belies their background. In some cases, such as the one depicted in *West Side Story*, a Puerto Rican accent may be sufficient to prevent Anita from acquiring the terrace apartment of her dreams.

In my case, due to my ability to style shift, I was able to conduct a series of experience to test this hypothesis; namely, might prospective landlords deny access to someone whose voice conveyed their racial background? Results found in research I conducted with colleagues in 1999 (Purnell *et al.*, 1999) confirm that the answer is an emphatic 'yes they can, and yes they did'. Briefly, the more affluent the community, the less likely someone whose voice sounded stereotypically Black or Latinx would be granted an appointment to view an apartment.

I wasn't the first one to really look at this issue; this had come up before. This is a scene from the movie *West Side Story* and there's a line in one of the songs that is directly related to the point I'm making. That was in 1960, I was 10 years old, so long before I was interested in that. But this movie wasn't the first time that this issue came up. It's in the Old Testament. Literally, the word Shibboleth has to do with this. Back in biblical times those that could not pronounce the word Shibboleth and pronounced it as 'Sibboleth' were killed.

What this also means is that their dress appearance and everything else about them was so similar that the only way to detect your enemy was through their pronunciation, so linguistic profiling is biblical in nature. But the way that I discovered it was that many people are discriminated against over the telephone unseen.

I therefore conducted experiments in the San Francisco Bay Area; my performance varied depending upon the relative affluence of the community and the dialect that I used to try to call to make an appointment. I got very different responses in East Palo Alto, Oakland and San Francisco communities where you have a significant number of minorities. Palo Alto and Woodside are predominantly White communities that are very affluent. Palo Alto and Woodside in Silicon Valley proper and East Palo Alto in Oakland are noteworthy because they have the majority of minority populations in those communities.

I grew up in Los Angeles. In Los Angeles, I would say *hello* when I'm calling about the apartment you have advertised in the paper. But other times I would say *hello you have advertised in the paper.* I used my ability to manipulate the different dialects and make different calls.

This resulted in different responses and exposed that linguistic profiling was significant and a barrier, not only to housing, but employment and other opportunities.

After that I got a lot of this work. I got called in for other trials; the one that I want to talk about right now is a wiretapped recording.

In the United States, if you get arrested and you make a telephone call from jail, it can be recorded and anything you say can be used in court against you. Law enforcement has the right to record any telephone conversation that occurs with an inmate. For the case in question, a recording made while a murder defendant was in jail was claimed by prosecutors to provide clear evidence of his guilt. According to the prosecutor, the African American murder defendant was heard to say, 'Why would I do a speedy trial when I know I committed this shit?' However, upon listening to the recording, the defendant said the opposite; namely, 'Why I'm a do a speedy trial when I know I ain'(t) committed this shit?'

From a purely linguistic point of view, the difference between an affirmative statement, admitting guilt, and a negative statement, denying guilt, is conveyed through a nasalized diphthong that would be difficult to hear during rapid, animated, speech. I therefore conducted some comparative spectrographic analyses with African American men whose linguistic backgrounds were somewhat similar to the defendant, asking them to produce two versions of the sentences in question; that is, 'I know I committed this shit' and 'I know I ain'(t) committed this shit'.

By comparing spectrographic analyses, slight differences could easily be seen, that might have been difficult to hear. As a result, the jury decided not to invoke the death penalty. The defendant was still found guilty, but the linguistic evidence was sufficient to raise the prospect that he might not be guilty, and if additional exculpatory evidence came to light at a future date, he would still be alive to have his case re-examined. Had he been put to death, there would be no possibility to overturn a potentially wrongful outcome.

The next case is quite horrible; one where a murder and an attempted murder occurred. In addition, the murder suspect ultimately decided to serve as his own attorney and defend himself at trial. The murder suspect was involved in gang activity in the city of Baltimore; he had a girlfriend that lived about three hours away by car in a town called Carlisle, Pennsylvania; they dated off and on for many years.

He sometimes appeared on the internet with guns, money and drugs. As such he did not hide the fact that he was involved in gang activity. Eventually the young woman he was dating broke up with him. However, he would show up at her apartment from time to time unannounced. She often let him come in, and some of those encounters resulted in intimacy, sometimes they did not. Eventually, a little bit of time went by and she met a new boyfriend whose background was very different. He had a good job. He was very active in his church. He was not involved with drugs or guns.

On the night in question she got off work late. Her new boyfriend got a pizza, picked her up from her place of work and went back to her apartment to watch a movie. Upon their arrival, the new boyfriend went upstairs to take a shower. While doing so, the old boyfriend – the murder suspect – arrived at the apartment unannounced. She let him in, whereupon he told her that he needed to talk with her, and she refused. She told him that she had company and could not talk at that time. He took umbrage and told her to tell her guest to leave; she refused. He then pulled out a gun and shot her in the neck; she hit the floor, bleeding profusely. He then went upstairs and discovered the new boyfriend, shooting him eight times while he was still taking a shower. He then went back downstairs, and stepped over her body as he left, presumably believing that she was dead.

However, after nearly 45 minutes, she gained consciousness and was able to drag herself to a neighbor's home. She was unable to speak, but she wrote down the name of the former boyfriend as her assailant, and he was then arrested for murder and attempted murder.

During his trial, he was given two public prosecutors; however, he did not think that the public prosecutors were helpful to him, so he asked the judge to please give him different public prosecutors. The judge refused and he then decided that he wanted to defend himself.

When he defended himself, however, he made a lot of mistakes during trial, not the least of which being that he was very honest to the all-White jury, claiming that many of the difficulties he had faced in life were as a result of mistreatment by White people. He told them that he wasn't a perfect angel throughout his life. He had faced a lot of difficulties, but none of those difficulties were greater than when he actually had to deal with White people.

While his candor was honest, he ultimately received a conviction and was sent back to jail. While he was awaiting his sentence, some independent evidence came to light that the judge in the trial, who was White, and the prosecuting attorney in the trial, who was also White, had been exchanging racist and homophobic emails on their work computers using pseudonyms. The murder suspect then decided that this new information confirmed that the judge and prosecutor were both racist, and incapable of being fair and impartial officers of the court. He wanted a new trial, only to be told that an appellate judge would review his case, to determine whether or not he had received a fair trial. The judge concluded that he had received a fair trial, while also acknowledging that the trial had not been 'perfect'.

The primary imperfection grew out of some hyperbolic statements made by the prosecutor during closing remarks, claiming that the defendant was a 'big city guy who had been disrespected'. Moreover, the appellate judge produced an opinion indicating that the jurors did not draw any racial inference from this statement. I was asked to evaluate the veracity of that claim, and ultimately demonstrated that a majority of disinterested parties did in fact draw significant racial inferences that the assertion that he was 'a big city guy who had been disrespected' was said primarily about an African American gang member. Some evaluators concluded that the phrase made reference to a Mafia boss; that is, a wealthy White gangster. Nevertheless, more than 75% of neutral evaluators believed the statement was made in reference to an inner-city African American gang member. Of great significance, these independent evaluations suggest that the appellate judge overstated his opinion regarding the benign racial characterization that he attributed to the prosecutor's depiction of 'a big city guy who was disrespected', thereby suggesting that the trial might have had racial bias. While the defendant may have been guilty of the crimes for which he was convicted, one would hope that he would be given a fair trial free of unwelcome racial innuendo.

The next case that I want to discuss also took place in the United States. In this instance, the question at hand has to do with the potential creation of a hostile work environment against a class of men, all of whom were born in Africa, and all of whom learned English as a second language. As such, each man who is part of this class-action lawsuit speaks English with a distinctive and recognizable African accent; it would be obvious to any native speaker of American English that English is not their first language, although they all speak and comprehend English fluently.

The trial centers on claims that the man who supervised these men, a White monolingual speaker of American English, employed racially charged language by routinely referring to these employees, all subordinates who are Black men, as

'monkeys'. In short, is it racist to call someone a monkey? Not necessarily; for example, if you tell someone to stop that 'monkey business', that's not necessarily racist.
If you say, don't throw a 'monkey wrench in it', that might not be racist either. Any
American parent, regardless of race, might tell their children that 'You "little monkeys" are real troublemakers!'

In his own defense, the White supervisor claimed that he was trying to motivate
the workers by saying that 'the job is so easy a monkey could do it'. Moreover, he
indicated that this statement was intended to motivate the workers, not humiliate
them. However, some additional evidence came to light that was problematic. The
supervisor was overheard asking one of the employees about his lunch: 'What is that
shit you're eating, monkey soup?'

During my testimony I was able to point out that the preceding quote is ambigu-
ous, but either interpretation is problematic from the standpoint of claiming that
such remarks did not result in a hostile, racially charged, work environment. One
interpretation is that 'monkey soup' is eaten by humans, and that it contains monkey
meat. The other interpretation is that 'monkey soup' is soup that is eaten by a
monkey, regardless of the ingredients that are used to make the soup. Either interpretation has a degrading interpretation, and when used exclusively to describe men
who were born in Africa, the racial connotations are inescapable.

I would like to close with a more uplifting story. Many readers will recall the
horrific attack on the twin towers in New York on September 11, 2001. At that time
I was a Professor at Stanford University, and I received a call from a woman who
asked me if I might be able to help her, and I said, in what way, and she said that she
had a legal problem.

She told me that she found my name on the internet, and she thought that I might
be able to help her with a legal case. She is an African American woman who lived
and worked in Oakland, California. Prior to her employment she had been a single
mother on welfare raising three children, doing all she could to escape poverty.
Eventually she obtained a good job with the city of Oakland, and she improved her
living circumstances for herself and her children.

After she obtained the job, she received a citation for a minor traffic violation.
On the day in question, she was standing in line at City Hall to pay her fine, and she
decided to do so during her lunch break. As such, her time was limited, and the line
was fairly long. As she waited, she realized a growing need to use the restroom – with
ever increasing urgency. Although she decided to wait in line, her need to relieve
herself intensified, so much so that she turned to an elderly White woman behind her,
exclaiming 'When I finish up at the window I'm going to drop a bomb in the bath-
room'. Again, this statement was made only weeks after the attack on the twin
towers, and the vast majority of Americans were far more sensitive about potential
threats, especially against potential governmental targets.

As she was seated in the ladies' room, the police burst into her occupied stall –
guns drawn, and she was arrested for having threatened to explode a bomb at City
Hall. While her financial circumstances had clearly improved, she was not wealthy,
and was given a public defender. He suggested that she admit guilt, telling her that
doing so would result in probation without jail time or the potential to become sepa-
rated from her children. He then pointed out that were she to go to trial, if she lost,

she would surely be incarcerated, and her children would be placed in foster care. It was under these stressful and dire circumstances that she contacted me, and shared her legal quandary.

I was able to submit a letter to the judge indicating that her statement about 'dropping a bomb' was not literal, but a euphemism intended to find a more polite way of describing her urgent need to defecate. I provided a few other examples of euphemisms, such as 'It's raining cats and dogs', or describing someone's death as 'kicking the bucket'. The judge dropped all charges, and she was able to continue her job without fear of a police record, which could have resulted in the loss of her job, and an unwelcome return to poverty and a life on welfare.

When she called and shared the good news of the favorable outcome of her trial, she asked me about compensation, 'What do I owe you?' After a brief moment of reflection, I told her that at some future date, as yet undetermined, she would find herself in circumstances where she would be able to help someone else in need. I simply asked her to pay it forward, and she told me she would be delighted to do so.

---

### Comments from the chat box

Dee Mohale: Thank you Prof
Betty Dlamini: Thank you Prof. This is amazing!
Hala: Thank you Professor!
Sopuruchi Aboh: Thank you Prof. for this insightful lecture.
abinro@auburn.edu: I used to teach language and the law but retired in 2018. I wish I'd had your book when I was teaching, Thank you John
Karen Keifer-Boyd (she, her): Thank you Dr. Baugh for your important work and fascinating presentation.
Katalin Egri Ku-Mesu: Wole Soyinka's poem 'Telephone Conversation' is an excellent illustration

---

### Lomeu Gomes

Thank you very much, Professor. It was really interesting to see such clear examples of how linguistic knowledge can be used to promote justice or to expose situations in which injustice happens. And I'd like to ask Makoni if you'd like to initiate the discussion.

### Makoni

I think what we'll do is let's open it up to everybody.

### Kanavillil Rajagopalan (University of Campinas, Brazil)

Hello, I'm Rajan from Brazil. I wonder if you would like to comment on the well-known fact that racial slurs work in virtue of their perlocutionary potential which is an idea from John Austin's speech – act theory. I've often wondered: what is the role of speech acts in your research into linguistic profiling?

## Baugh

Yeah, yeah, that's a very important point. And thank you very much for reminding me of Austin's work which I read many years ago. So you're actually talking about the crucial issue of what it all boiled down to. In that particular trial, right, because in fact it was a hung jury.

On the very grounds that you say some of the jurors said that, you know, the man that made the comments intended no offense whatsoever. My role which came up more in the second trial, it had to do with that specific sentence that was uttered about monkey. What's that 'shit' you're eating right, so there we had the added advantage he referred to the food as 'shit', right and even, so that's derogatory, right. 'Shit' is not anything that anyone would commonly eat, so when you take that particular utterance, in the context of this trial, it's very damaging to the defendant because of other instances where he commonly referred to these workers as monkeys. It was the overall cumulative usage of that derogatory term that made the point, but you're, you're absolutely right about the issue of racial slur.

The second issue is one of intentionality. Right. So here in the United States right now there's a common phrase called 'dog whistle'. We're in the midst of a very heated election. A lot of these issues are controversial and I agree with you. The impact is often on the person who's the recipient exactly. The question comes into play. How much power do they have in addressing it?

## Rajagopalan

Thank you very much. Thank you.

## Ofelia García (The Graduate Center, City University of New York)

I just wanted to say how nice it is to see you after so many years. I wanted you to discuss a bit the relationship between your work and the white listening subject work of Nelson Flores and Jonathan Rosa.

## Baugh

How wonderful to see you again as well. You know, I've been through all of my training. So, I'm not supposed to tell you how wonderful you look. But why don't you tell the audience a little bit about the work of, you know, Flores, and Rosa, and then I'll pick it up after that.

## García

Yeah, I just think it's so interesting because both you and them have worked from different perspectives in a lot of ways. I'm your generation. Your work was trailblazing in terms of linguistic discrimination and its impact is very obvious. Their work stems more from an ideological perspective. But I think, in a way, your work and theirs are related and it may say something about generational differences and maybe where we are today, because I do think, like you said, we're at a very difficult time but we are also at a time of more racial consciousness, more engagement with race and Black Lives Matter.

And so I'm just thinking that the way in which you approached your work at your time is not the way that they're approaching their work in their time, and yet I see this idea of the white listening subject very present in your work also.

## Baugh

Right, so that's a, that's a good point. So I want to say a little bit more about that. So for those who don't already know the work of Nelson Flores and Jonathan Rosa. They are younger scholars, Flores at the University of Pennsylvania, Jonathan Rosa is at Stanford University. And they both coined the terminology *raciolinguistics* to talk about linguistic analysis where the issue of race was fundamentally embedded, rightly so, whereas sociolinguistics or anthropological linguistics is connected to a discipline. Raciolinguistics as developed by those two scholars always tries to bring racial issues to the fore, and there's a book by Jonathan Rosa (2018) which he titles *Looking Like a Language, Sounding Like a Race*. Where our work intersects has to do with stereotypes that are associated with racial groups of people. In different parts of the world different races are associated with distinctive manners of speaking.

And it isn't always the case that there's a one-to-one alignment between a person's racial background and their manner of speaking, but in societies where racial segregation exist, you tend to find different linguistic groupings that have distinctive characteristics that can be identified in one way or another. So, our work does overlap in many ways, but I just wasn't smart enough to think of raciolinguistics first, so good for them for doing that and bringing important focus to it.

## García

Nelson was my student, and I know their interest is on raciolinguistic ideologies. They're not interested in pointing to the fact that language characteristics are systemic or normed. They're interested in looking at the ideologies that we all hold when we listen. And I think there is a shift between thinking of the speaker, which is what sociolinguistics has always thought about even when we have defended differences, and the Flores/Rosa approach which poses it as an ideology of listeners. No matter how systemic our language is, if people perceive you as being different, they will have these ideologies about you and your language. So, I see that there is a change, although there's a coming together. Younger people have this different theoretical framework now, which you and I did not have when we started out.

## Stephanie Rudwick (University of Hradec Králové, Czech Republic)

To pick up on what has been said earlier, there is an argument that suggests that language, or at least the definition of excellence (mostly in English), downplays issues of race. So perhaps sometimes language can blur certain racial constructions. But at the same time, the opposite can also happen, it can create racial dynamics within the same racial group.

The kind of anecdotes you've been talking about, e.g. flat hunting in the USA, they are also relevant in South Africa, for instance in Cape Town. It's incredibly difficult for people who speak with a strong Black South African English accent to rent places. And then, the other issue really is that language might get you through – so you might have the linguistic capacity to actually pass as a White person but as soon as you get to the venue, you still find that it's race which disqualifies you. So, with these intersections of language and race, there is a limit to what language can do for you as a person of colour. This question needs further attention: where are the limits of language against the power of race?

I would like to just hear from someone like you how we can push further on these issues, let's say the ontology of how we think about language as opposed to how we think about race, where we can really push the field further. In terms of racial linguistics, I think I sometimes struggle because the field is extremely US dominated and certain issues do not apply in South Africa, for instance. I really found the works in *Black Linguistics* (Makoni *et al.*, 2002) pioneering; for me that is in many ways much more valuable than some of the new work that has been coming out.

## Baugh

Okay, thanks for that question. So, I've spent a fair amount of time in South Africa and have had the interesting experience of being in different cities in your country and, you know, people walk up to me and immediately speak Afrikaans, right, just based on my appearance and as soon as I start to speak, then they can hear I'm an American. And there's a different reaction. The points that you're raising are incredibly important.

I don't know your country as well as I would like, but it's an evolutionary process. When I compare the South African situation to the situation in the US, in some ways because the United States is a country that also has its own history of apartheid and, where it's different, is that the United States was much more destructive to the Indigenous populations. We've never had a Native American president, you've all had Mandela.

And that's because of the fact that Blacks are still a majority in South Africa; Native Americans are a small minority in the United States. Right. Some of what I want to say, also I think applies to Australia and New Zealand.

To a certain extent you're seeing that race and language are closely aligned. I think I'm going to try to keep this brief and only say that I recognize the problem that you're identifying. There are certain limits that linguistic science can bring to this just based on constraints on the tools that are in that science. I don't want to oversell it.

For example, I'm very critical of some forensic linguists who make claims that they can detect when people are lying, right, so we don't want to oversell what we can do, but I don't want to undersell it either. I think that in many instances, when race and language are used in tandem for discriminatory purpose there's, there's a lot to be said for working in harmony with political scientists and economists and, for that matter, medical professionals. I mean, in the United States we see racial differences and health disparities based on allocations to medications and even more so.

My book *Linguistics in Pursuit of Justice* (Baugh, 2018) talks about how the science of linguistics can help to address some dimensions of that, but it has to be worked. It's interdisciplinary as you mentioned, to be successful.

I want to use an illustration from the work I get on housing discrimination that just raises the specter of how sophisticated we need to be to address the political concerns you're raising; when I first did the work on linguistic profiling and housing, and unfair housing, I was not only proud of that work, but actually thought that it would make a difference in certain policies and it did. These issues were introduced in court and there were different circumstances where we were very successful, but there was another thing that I hadn't anticipated that was really problematic.

So, for example, prior to the work that I did it was very common for many real-estate agents who were discriminating against minorities to refuse to give them applications to see apartments or deny them appointments to see apartments. After I did the work, the racist landlords became aware of it and they got more sophisticated in their discrimination. What happened is they would let Black people come see an apartment, they would take an application and then they would throw it in the trash, so in the political arena, we have to be sophisticated enough to know that the positive things that we're trying to contribute may be… We have to watch out for the instances where they can be weaponized against us. But thank you for that important question.

So while you're trying to unmute I can see the one about President Trump's comments about Africa that were just so offensive. You know, but it's, it goes to the previous question in terms of the political climate in which we live. Those of us that are familiar with Donald Trump and his career, know that he was, he and his father were notorious in New York for denying opportunities for Black people to live in apartments that they have, right? The racial discrimination was so much that they actually got taken to court for it and President Trump has known that racial bigots within the United States, that he wants their votes, right, in addition to what he said about you know his derogatory comments about African nations recently came up in Michael Cohen's book. President Trump asked Michael Cohen, do you know of any countries in the world that are led by Blacks? At that time Barack Obama was president. He said, what about the United States to which President Trump responded with, you know, profanity, right, so unfortunately, there are people who will exploit the racism within the United States and the disparaging comments that he made about Africa and denying Nigerians opportunities to get visas to travel to the United States. That's, that's, again, part of both the 'dog whistle' of racism and overt racism, right, so it's a clear instance of racial profiling.

### Lynn Mario de Souza (University of São Paulo, Brazil)

Professor Baugh, I'm speaking from the University of São Paulo, Brazil. I'd like to come back to the comment that Ofelia made referring to the work of Flores and Rosa and the fact that racism may be ideological and systemic. Here I'm speaking from the perspective of Brazil where racism is structural and systemic. This means that it's very difficult to talk about intentionality because what we have is a kind of normalized distributed intentionality on the part of perpetrators. When racism is brought up it's generally by the victims of racism and they get accused of being racist because they are pointing out racism which 'doesn't exist' because when you speak from the perspective of the system where racism is normalized we have this normalized, distributed intentionality which denies racism at the same time as it is practiced. It then becomes very difficult to fight against racism. So what I'm just saying is, to what extent do you think we can talk about racism in general, without looking at how racism actually is ideologically embedded or systematized in particular contexts?

## John Baugh

I'm going to ask you to actually say a little bit more about that, based on your own observations in Brazil, and then after you finish, I'd like Ofelia to follow up because she, you know, was the one that raised those other issues. So, tell us a little bit more about the Brazilian situation and how you would answer your own question first.

## de Souza

Okay. So, for example, the current academics who are studying the issue of racism or colonization, not only in Brazil, but in Latin America in general, point to the fact that racism may not be a cause of anything, it may actually be the effect of the whole colonial system and the capitalist system of trading slaves and the later identification of inferiority or justification of exploiting another human being in terms of race. Race can then actually be seen as an effect and not as the cause (of racism). So when race is an effect and not the cause, the cause historically permeates the whole system, which is the justification and origin of the cause, which all results in a perceived inferiority. Inequality then becomes normalized without the word race coming up. So, when race comes up more recently, in opposition to the system which normalized inequality, then racism is commonly turned back against whoever points to or denounces (institutionalized, systematic) racism.

## Baugh

Okay, so Brazil is a very different situation still, right? Because when we talk about the US and South Africa in the nature of discrimination... Bob Woodward asked President Trump explicitly whether or not he knew that White men have privileged backgrounds. That they may not be able to really empathize with the plight of Black Americans and President Trump said, oh, I don't see that at all. You know, there's no such thing as systematic racism or systemic racism in the United States.

So, when you look at just the broad spectrum of the full political diversity, it's ironic. But a true thing is that the victims of discrimination are often blamed, and especially when they bring it up, and in Brazil, I think it's even more the case. I mean, you know, you've gone through your own political turmoils and swings from, you know, Lula to your current president and, you know, so it's a country where democracy also represents, you know, people from very, very diverse backgrounds, and I think the racism in Brazil is in some ways even more complex than it is in the places that have historically had more overt forms of apartheid.

### Joseph Igono (Federal University Lafia, Nigeria)

My question is to what extent can we use your work here in Nigeria. There are issues about social justice but they are not related to race but more to do with issues about ethnic diversity.

### Baugh

Thank you for your question. And that's really a very important one. When I first began the work and most of the discussion we've had today has been focused on situations where we're looking at linguistic discrimination and multi-racial societies.

But I often ask people to do a thought experiment in the US context pretending that there's no racial diversity and that the entire population is of European descent. And if everyone in the United States was still White, would there be linguistic discrimination and people say, oh, yes, there would, it would be different based on region and class. Other differences would come into play. So in Nigeria, you see, you know, a linguistic situation where the divisions based on language, based on class, based on education and opportunity, can result in discrimination and what we do... the work is also very similar. There would be situations where some groups think that their language is either superior to others or that other groups are inferior to them and, to the extent possible, we try to navigate, renegotiate through linguistic research efforts to promote greater opportunities and make people aware that all languages and dialects in the world are equal. But I really want to thank you for that question because linguistic discrimination far exceeds race in many societies and that's very important.

### Sibusiso Cliff Ndlangamandla (University of South Africa)

I was just thinking that the field, it appears to be centered around monolingualism whereas here in South Africa, we have issues of service delivery, which are normally taken up by people with more resources and maybe people who don't speak the language, the official language or English, so to say. I wanted to find out how does forensic linguistics operate in those spaces and also technological spaces and/ or multi-modality and multi-literacy.

### Baugh

Yeah, that's another fantastic question. And I want to thank you very much for that. So, going back to the South African situation. A lot of people may not know this, but Raj Mesthrie from Cape Town was actually one of my students, many years ago, when he attended graduate school at the University of Texas at Austin.

You know, I learned a lot about the situation in South Africa before getting there from Raj Mesthrie. When I finally got there, I was lucky enough to meet Neville Alexander and to, you know, work closely enough with Neville Alexander as he was trying to develop the new national language policy.

And so, ironically, this question exposes both ways in which South Africa is ahead of the rest of the world with respect to their national language policy and also the challenges that still exist when English and Afrikaans still have a privileged position because of their historical legacy as being the first official languages, right? So, to Neville Alexander's credit, I think one of the important things was not to eliminate either English or Afrikaans as official languages, there are practical reasons why you don't do that. But the challenge that the country still faces is trying to elevate all the other official languages. And that's not to mention the fact that there are still other languages, right? It is truly a complex multi-lingual country, I think South Africa has been a leader in terms of the rest of the world, paying attention to an important thing that you did across languages was the Truth and Reconciliation Commission. The world had never seen anything like that.

You know, the United States is a multilingual country, but if you show up in a courtroom here and English is not your native language, you're at a great disadvantage. And I know that the questioner is concerned about some of that. What we have to try to do is to use our abilities to make sure that individuals from diverse backgrounds obtain the highest education possible. Also, it may be necessary for those individuals to become bilingual, not only in their Indigenous language, but in one of the dominant languages so that they can then navigate the power structure.

---

### Comments from the chat box

Kanavillil: Thank you all. Very enjoyable session!
Karien van den Berg: Thank you so much for an engaging discussion John and everyone else!
Mark Visona: Thank you Dr Baugh and to the organizers!!

---

## References

Austin, J.L. (1975) *How to Do Things with Words*. Oxford: Oxford University Press.

Makoni, S., Smitherman, G., Ball, A.F. and Spears, A.K. (eds) (2002) *Black Linguistics: Language, Society and Politics in Africa and the Americas*. London and New York: Routledge.

Purnell, T., Idsardi, W. and Baugh, J. (1999) Perceptual and phonetic experiments on American English dialect identification. *Journal of Language and Social Psychology* 18 (1), 10–30.

Baugh, J. (2018) *Linguistics in Pursuit of Justice*. Cambridge: Cambridge University Press.

Rosa, J. (2018) *Looking Like a Language, Sounding Like a Race: Raciolinguistic Ideologies and the Learning of Latinidad*. New York: Oxford University Press.

# Epilogue: Transcending Metonymic Reason: Foregrounding Southern Coordinates of Sociolinguistic Thought and Rethinking Academic Cultures

Bassey E. Antia

Several anecdotes come to mind as one thinks about how partial knowledge can be made to potentially exhaust the infinite possibilities of knowledges, or just how liberating it can ultimately be for one to recognize and to transcend such flagrant incompleteness.

The story is also told of mother duck waiting for her brood to hatch. As one shell after another cracks, the young ducks step out into the world. As they take in the environment around the nest, they are struck by just how large the world is. The comparison is of course to the eggshell they have just come out from. 'Do you imagine this is the whole world?' asks the mother. 'Wait till you have seen the garden; it stretches far beyond that to the parson's field, but I have never ventured to such a distance' (Andersen, n.d.).

The story is also told of a Western anthropologist who had been studying an African group. At the end of his research stay and just moments before he departs, the anthropologist gets a group of children to race, with the promise that the winner would be rewarded with a basket of fruits at the finish line. With the '*Go!*' cue, the children, rather unexpectedly, hold each other's hands and run together towards the finish line. They arrive together and they all share the prize. The puzzled anthropologist, for whom individualism and competition were universally feted ideals, asks what had just happened. A little girl explains that it was inconceivable for one person to be happy while the others were sad. The reward was in the collectively shared experience of the fruity treat (Olive Network, n.d.).

In the former story, the message from mother duck to the young ducks is clear: what there is to know about the world is not exhausted by your vision – not yours, not mine, not anyone's. The latter anecdote teaches a lesson in philosophical alterity, a lesson in *Ubuntu* – which is one traditional African concept of mutual dependence and solidary ontology.

These lessons all resonate with the plea for *shifting the geography of reason* as elaborated on by Gordon (2021) or the construct of *lazy reason* in work by de Sousa Santos (2016), but also with the *hubris of zero point epistemology* as proposed by Castro-Gómez, discussed by Mignolo (2011). Like the narratives, these theoretical formulations all tackle hegemonic reason and vision: they point to the limitations of hegemonic knowledges; they query the passing off as universal and neutral what is in fact provincial, biased, imperial and sexist; they invite an ethics of knowledge production and consumption in which positional coordinates are declared; they accentuate the need for a critical historiography of knowledge production, at least until such a time (if ever) positional self-declaration becomes standard operating procedure in scholarship both in the Global South and indeed in the Global North as well.

Shifting the geography of reason is about recognising other positionalities, for example, the ideologically construed Global South, as legitimate perspectives for the production of reason. Reason from Southern coordinates may stand in different kinds of relations with hegemonic Northern reason, which produced but has also been sustained by capitalism, colonialism, racism, slavery and sexism (Gordon, 2021; Mignolo, 2011). Southern reason may denounce Northern reason as unreasonable or as no reason at all; it may particularize Northern reason and position it as one of several legitimate reasons; or, quite significantly, it may create new knowledges without the stifling entrapment and decadent strictures of what is currently known in the North, in a process of *teleological suspension of disciplinarity* (Gordon, 2021).

Lazy reason is de Sousa Santos's term for a deprecated rationality, the one that undergirds a hegemonic Northern view of the world. Lazy reason assumes that the North's understanding of the world exhausts all possible or legitimate understandings; that there is one conception (linear) of time; and that the present (time) has to be contracted and experiences associated with it can go to waste. Of course, the North, although often associated with the West and its modernity, need not necessarily be seen in geographic terms. Neither should the South, associated with resistance to hegemonic power and/or the articulation of an independent rationality.

The girl in the anecdote is Gordon's precursor. They both draw attention to the existence of other positional coordinates of reason beyond what our capacity or socialization allows us to apprehend. Mother duck is also de Sousa Santos' precursor. They both suggest that a single angle of vision does not exhaust the infinity of potential visions. There are different knowledges to be known, and infinite ways of knowing an item knowledge. As the Igbo of Southeast Nigeria say, 'otu onye tuo izu, o gbue ochu' (knowledge is never complete/never resides in one person: two heads are better than one).

In a sense, the foregoing provides a sketch of the sort of conversations into which the Global Forum at Pennsylvania State University, USA, has inserted itself. Led by Sinfree Makoni, this truly global forum engages in conversation with scholars as a means to 'decenter hegemonic epistemologies and to decolonize the Western canon to facilitate other ways/waves of knowing', as the vision statement of the Forum puts it. This volume, which contains the first five conversations in the series, foreshadows for the reader the sorts of lively engagements in the close to 100 other conversations that have taken place to date. Each presenter is invited to participate on the basis of a particular publication, which serves as an entry point for the speaker and the audience.

The first chapter of the volume is based on a conversation with South Africa-based Kwesi Prah, an anthropologist, a political activist, a linguist, a true pan-African who has taught in many parts of Africa (Ghana, Sudan, Lesotho, South Africa). He discusses the university in Africa and the nexus of language and development in Africa. He is the author of, among many other books, *The Challenge of Decolonizing Education* (CASAS, 2018). Through its work on harmonising the orthographies of clusters of languages in Africa, the Centre for Advanced Studies of African Society (CASAS) of which he is the founding director has over some two decades debunked the colonially interpellated myth of Africa being a Tower of Babel. From their Canadian location, privileged yet peripheral in the American empire, Monica Heller and Bonnie McElhinny in the second chapter discuss citation practices, sociolinguistics, and conceptualizations of language. Linguists of multiple persuasions, they are the authors of *Language, Capitalism, Colonialism: Toward a Critical History* (University of Toronto Press, 2017), among others. In the third chapter, Hong Kong-based Chris Hutton (linguist, lawyer, and a buff of intellectual history) offers a kaleidoscope of perspectives on what it means to think laterally about linguistics, drawing in part from the work of the iconoclast, philosopher, linguist Roy Harris. Hutton underscores the importance of being acutely aware of the social, ideological and political entanglements of the discipline, and of constantly historicising disciplinary concepts. Hutton is the author of several books, including *Linguistics and the Third Reich: Mother-tongue Fascism, Race and the Science of Language* (Routledge, 1999).

In the fourth chapter, British-born, US-based Robbie Shilliam, a political scientist, examines multiple dimensions of the Black experience at universities in multiple geolocations, bringing into sharp relief in the process how apparent diversity may occlude the much-needed work of decolonisation that is central to dismantling the colonial matrices of power. Shilliam is the author of *The Black Pacific: Anti-colonial Struggles and Oceanic Connections* (Bloomsbury, 2015) and of the 2019 article, 'Behind the Rhodes statue: Black competency and the imperial academy', which appeared in *History of the Human Sciences* 32 (5), 3–27. Finally, in the fifth chapter, John Baugh reflects on a life-long career in forensic linguistics, which has seen him deploy his expertise to combatting injustice in various social domains, and especially within the US (criminal) justice system, which disproportionally discriminates against people of colour. John Baugh is the author of *Linguistics in Pursuit of Justice* (Cambridge University Press, 2018).

Over and beyond the fact of these conversations appearing within Makoni's Global Forum series, which *ipso facto* presupposes thematic relevance vis-à-vis the goals of the Forum, the delicate ideological work the conversations coherently perform, as well as how they feed into wider conversations of de/coloniality, still need to be demonstrated. Coordinates for plotting my reading may or not be inferred from my background in sociolinguistics; a peripatetic studentship; my antecedents in academic union politics in Nigeria; my interest in higher education management; my location in a historically Black university in South Africa – the one country on the continent of Africa that has recently witnessed a resurgence of interest in decolonising the academy; and my role as a co-moderator of Makoni's Global Forum series.

On my reading, *metonymic reason* – its logics, manifestations, consequences, and the imperatives of a response – is the common thread running through these chapters. Metonymic reason is de Sousa Santos's term for a type of lazy reason. It evinces a most brazen enactment of power. An important hallmark of Western modernity, it has a warped obsession with the whole or totality. It is egregiously warped because 'the whole is indeed a part turned into a term of reference for others' (de Sousa Santos, 2016: 167). Other parts are needed only to serve as backdrop against which the virtues of the preferred piece are extolled. The conceptual or rhetorical move is a familiar one, and is easily described as contractive accommodation (in contrast to expansive accommodation); in other words, accommodating only to silence (Antia & van der Merwe, 2019: 413). While dichotomies (e.g. scientific/traditional, culture/nature, White/Black, Europe/Africa, man/woman) proliferate in metonymic reason, and create an impression of symmetry, this symmetry is only a smokescreen for intended hierarchical relations.

The notion that sense can only be made in relation to a whole which is no more than a privileged part could mean the following: first, that the resulting understanding of the world is partial or selective; second, and more perniciously, that the understanding is also the outcome of relations of power, of an active and a ruthless subversion of other rationalities through whose fabricated nonexistence the privileged part comes into full splendor. 'Nonexistence', de Sousa writes, 'is produced whenever a certain entity is disqualified and rendered invisible, unintelligible, or irreversibly discardable' (de Sousa Santos, 2016: 172). He argues further that 'reality cannot be reduced to what exists because what exists is only the visible part of reality that modern abyssal thinking defines as being on this side of the line' (2016: 172).

Interestingly, and central to an accounting for the chapters in this volume, is de Sousa Santos' view that there is not one way, but several ways, of fabricating nonexistence – all of which have a common origin in a monoculture of reason. A monoculture of knowledge (rigor) holds up certain canons of what constitutes knowledge. Nonexistent knowledge is candidate knowledge that falls short of these lofty canons, and has to consequently contend with a subsidiary status as superstition, field notes, belief or opinion – irrespective of the civilisations it has supported over millennia. A hegemonic monoculture of social classification sets up categories to which people are then assigned on the basis of differences which have putative indexicalities that are held up to be natural. Demographic nonexistence is interpellated, quite naturally, by fabricated insuperable inferiority.

A monoculture of the dominant scale holds up specific orientations to contexts or space as the gold standard. This standard provides justification for non-conforming scalar orientations to be irremediably condemned. Western modernity is said to privilege universalism and globalization – lenses through which the local or the particular is refigured as incapacitation and incompetence. It is of course forgotten that the universal is a local powered by hegemonic forces. A monoculture of temporality recognises only linear time with discrete points that are read unidirectionally when determinations are made of what constitutes progress or its levels. Schedule time and monochronic time orientations are privileged. Enacted as nonexistent are those ways of being and forms of progress and being that are characterised by multiple temporalities, different modes of contemporaneity, polychronous time orientations, or event time. Finally, a monoculture of capitalist productivity is one that narrowly (non-sustainably) defines growth, privileges maximum profit/yield in the shortest turn-around times, sets a premium on non-solidary modes consistent with competition. Classified as nonproductive, thus unworthy of acknowledged existence, are modes of work that attend to sustainability concerns, and seek a balance among, for instance, profit, planet and people.

The response to the monocultures of metonymic reason, not surprisingly, lies in what de Sousa Santos sees as a corresponding set of ecologies. An ecology of knowledge expansively accommodates knowledges and ways of knowing; an ecology of recognition acknowledges difference but does not equate it with inequality; an ecology of trans-scale commits to what is uniquely local and uses this, when needed, as counterweight to an imagined and effacing universalism; an ecology of temporalities for instance validates a view of reality as a palimpsest of times; and an ecology of productivities admits of solidary conceptions of growth that are, therefore, compatible with equality of all kinds.

In their treatment of cross-cutting themes, for example, language or the university, the five chapters of this volume provide evidence for several of these logics or social forms of nonexistence as well as possible responses to them. Significantly, the chapters flesh out the dynamics of these logics in several ways, among others, by underscoring the point that reality-contracting metonymic reason operates through an interaction of these monocultures, rather than through independent modalities.

In what follows, I distil seven talking points across two areas, language and the university. With respect to language, many of the points distilled reiterate the earlier argument about the need for and relevance of a critical historiography of language study.

(1) There is discussion about how knowledge of languages in Northern centres conceals its Southern peripheral sources, and it may justly be asked to what extent the warrants for such erasure or invisibilisation of the periphery have to do with the canons of what is acknowledgeable/attributable knowledge, or the valuation of the sites and persons that supply such knowledge. To what extent are the Indian origins of phonetics or the notion of (multilingual) repertoire acknowledged? To what extent does the terminology of field notes acknowledge that the invaluable knowledge contained in such notes is in fact yanked off a well-developed and thriving intellectual tradition? To what extent is the putative global multilingual turn depicted as the Global North overcoming its one-language-nation-state legacy and coming to terms with what has in Africa and Asia always been a matter of course and a fact of life?

(2) The need to undo a monoculture of universal scale, in order to foster an ecology of knowledge and to legitimise local scales, is also underscored in the book. It is so easy to unquestioningly accept both the universal reach and/or the progressive import of such concepts as mother tongue, native language, native speaker, intuition, non-native speaker, and so on. As it turns out, an approach to the discipline that is characterised

by lateral thinking reveals that there are specific provincial intellectual histories associated with concepts such as these; that these concepts need not be used in every context; *ipso facto*, the use of other concepts that are more appropriate should enrich the knowledge ecology; and that, depending on context, fascism, racism and commodification may well be part of the baggage of these universalised concepts.

In a recent talk in the series, John Joseph draws attention to Western historical/ philosophical views of language. One embodied view of language is captured in Everardus Alemannus's 13th-century representation of 'lactating Lady Grammar', which is probably one early origin or early representation of the genetic-*cum*-gendered notion of the mother tongue. The universalisation of this particular gendered conceptualisation of language (or what is construed as a first language) has the effect of erasing local conceptualisations. To exemplify with groups and languages in Nigeria, for the Andoni or the Igala the traditional conceptualisation is of the father tongue; for the Bade or Epeye, reference is made to place; the Efik combine place and birth as they speak of 'usem isoñ emana' (the language of the land of my birth) (Brann, 1980). In the universalisation of one local, gendered conceptualisation, there is at one level perhaps an unknowing transfer or take-over of a specific historical view of language and its association with loyalty/fidelity, territory, purity (e.g. in antisemitic Nazi Germany). Of course, the notion taken over could very well be the Lutheran, democratic, anti-establishment one. In either sample scenarios, there is possibly an overwriting of other understandings and traditions, as well as a shutting down of possible research and interpretative options. This historical insight is liberating as it provides a warrant for unabashed local appropriations.

(3) From reading the book, it may be inferred how a monoculture of language knowledge, influenced in part by positivism in Western intellectual history but sustained always by unequal power relations, occluded other ways of experiencing language and impoverished the knowledge ecology associated with language study. It would be recalled that in the Western dialogue with nature, especially between the 17th and 19th centuries, nature was apprehended in ways that tended towards predictability, absoluteness, determinism, etc. (Antia, 2007: xiii). Objects of study had to be extracted from the messiness and entanglements in the lay experience and organised into tree diagrams and other hierarchies, again in contrast to 'common-sense knowledge which can tolerate – indeed, depends on – compromises, contradictions and indeterminacies of all kinds' (Halliday & Martin, 1993: 6). Not to be left behind in the race for the status of positivist science, linguistics embraced a reification of language and its enumerability (Makoni, 2003; Makoni & Pennycook, 2005) and developed corresponding tools and metalanguage.

The convenient exclusion of multispecies communication then reduced to superstition experiences such as those of the child narrator in Camara Laye's novel, *The African Child*:

> But as I have told you, my father kept moving his lips! We could hear those words, those secret words, those incantations which he addressed to powers that we should not, that we could not hear or see: this was essential. Only my father was versed in the science of conjuring the spirits of fire, air and gold, and conjuring evil spirits…
> (1959: 27)

When he [little black snake] was within reach, my father would stroke him with his hand, and the snake would accept the caress with a quivering of his whole body [...]. That caress, and the answering tremor – but I ought to say: that appealing caress and that answering tremor – threw me each time into an inexpressible confusion: I would imagine I know not what mysterious conversation... the hand inquired, and the tremor replied... Yes, it was like a conversation. Would I, too, converse like that one day? No: I was still attending the school. (Laye, 1959: 21)

The child narrator is not in doubt about there being a science and a legitimate conversation, but the question raised is whether mainstream scientific study of language shares or has traditionally shared these characterisations.

Against this backdrop, it is easy to see how a Southern epistemological pushback on Northern positivism via a number of ongoing initiatives is broadening the knowledge ecology and exemplifying Gordon's *teleological suspension of disciplinarity*. Metaphorical visualisations of language – as water, entangled electric wire, mangrove, rhizome – or approaches to its study – assemblages, integrationism, translanguaging – are different and welcome attempts at re-placing language at the crossroads of complexity from which it was extracted by professional linguistics, and to open it up for forms of study and understanding foreclosed by the orthodoxy that has prevailed for over a century.

Water, the rhizome, the mangrove, assemblages – these all become ways of conceptualising the limitless opportunities associated with language: its ontologies; its collective ownership as a commons; the alliances it forges and that are forged within it; what supports it or what it supports when deployed in communication; the metalanguage for its description; its human and non-human participants; why hermeneutic rather than hermetic conceptualisations may be more appropriate for its study and why its expansiveness limits the usefulness of attempts to contain it in one descriptive frame.

(4) The relationship between language and a politics of racial nonexistence discussed in the book contributes to our understanding of the burgeoning area of language and social justice as well as language and race. Among others, the reader is invited to consider how a politics of nonexistence in social domains is premised on the essentialisation of the links between a monoculture of classification (e.g. racial self- and other-positioning) and a monoculture knowledge (of language behaviours), such that there are reciprocal indexicalities between them. As a consequence of such essentialisation, language behaviours become the basis for and/or the visible marker of race-based discrimination in education, urban housing, or employment. Paradoxically, individuals with a command of a vast repertoire of speaking styles are able to game the system, even if for a fleeting moment, and to lay bare the processes through which racism fabricates nonexistence.

Significantly, in the justice system, much more than norms of appropriateness or acceptability of language use underlie the perceptive hegemony of what has been called the *white listening subject* (Flores & Rosa, 2015). White is a metaphor for power and does not always mean skin tone. In the criminal justice system, life and death issues are literally involved in the interpretive processes of the powerful listening subject. An ideologically tainted listening subject may choose to hear a George

Floyd say 'I ate too many drugs' rather than 'I ain't do no drugs'. We would, arguably, not be dealing here with noise in perception. For all we know, the alternate option may have been the only one allowed by the listening subject if a George Floyd were in a different relationship of power.

Let us now turn to the university. There are also several talking points around the ways in which hegemonic institutional academic practices and cultures fabricate forms of nonexistence.

(5) We are encouraged to view aspects of the histories and mandates of universities in the Global South as serving metropolitan or Northern hegemonies. The widespread reality of the university in Africa, rather than the African university, is historically tied to the dual mandate informing the founding of these institutions, summed up as follows: develop the native while attending to the interests of the empire. But this duality is in fact arguable as the early curricular offerings (e.g. classics) sought to (un)develop the native in ways that served imperial interests. While aspirations or pressures towards an international scale have shaped universities in the Global North as well, in the Global South these have been experienced as, or have translated into, a form of social disengagement with the local (and its knowledge). Decades ago, Ali Mazrui wrote the following while deploring the scholar and the university in Africa:

> On one side is the individual scholar and on the other the universe of international scholarship. What is often missing [in Africa] is the intermediate category of the particular society within which the scholar operates. The university is therefore either sub-social in its commitment or supra-social – but seldom adequately social. (Mazrui, 1978: 211)

Neither an international aspiration nor a plea for academic freedom is acceptable rationale for social disengagement. Kwame Nkrumah, pan-Africanist and Ghana's first president, wrote tellingly as follows in a 1963 speech at the University of Ghana:

> True academic freedom – the intellectual freedom of the university – is everywhere fully compatible with service to the community: for the university is and must always remain, a living, thinking and serving part of the community to which it belongs. (Nkrumah, 1969: 58)

The contemporary orientation of the university in Africa towards a global scale is, therefore, not without historical precedent. The revolutionary imagination of a recent generation of students clamouring for a multilevel decolonisation of universities continues the critique of Nkrumah, Ngugi wa Thiong'o, J.F. Ajayi, Chinweizu, Mazrui and, well before them, James Africanus Horton, Edward Wilmot Blyden and J.E. Casley-Hayford who had visions of an African, non-colonial university (Chinweizu, 1975: 324–327). Given that the historical dual mandate has probably morphed into something else today, it is legitimate to inquire into the altruism behind the agenda of a universal scale to which universities in the Global South are encouraged to orient today in the name of internationalisation, ranking systems, and so on.

Given centre-periphery disparities that account for a lopsided directionality in the flow of scholars, the use of non-local faculty quota at an institution in Africa as a measure of internationalisation and *ipso facto* ranking, does raise questions, as do, by the way, the non-disaggregation of research output according to gender or expatriate vs. local faculty, and so on. Because internationalisation is a criterion of many ranking systems, and league tables are marketed as indispensable, unfounded imperatives of a response have seen many an institution unthinkingly orient towards strategy and policy formulation in which the local is sacrificed on the altar of the international. In sum, the argument is that African universities cannot be established internationally if they seek to address international problems first. They must first seek to address local problems and then international status will take care of itself. An African proverb has it that you do not enter your house through someone else's door.

(6) We also infer from the book how a monoculture of classification raises questions of who is cognitively competent, how such competence is expected to be demonstrated, and who has what place in the academy and under what conditions – all of which have an effect on whether it is an ecology of knowledges that is fostered or a monoculture. Asking why the curriculum is so White or my reading list is only made up of male authors is a corollary of the politics of nonexistence in academia.

As it turns out, the initial curricular offerings in classics in universities in Africa from the 1940s may not have been that dissimilar from the embrace of such courses by Black students in the US from the 1860s. Probably underwriting the imposition of the discipline of Greco-Roman classics in one case, and its embrace in the other, is the same egregiously conceived rite of passage into humanity; in other words, the same concern around having those classified as belonging in a zone of non-being having to prove their claims to humanity through their ability to reason in prescribed ways.

Paradoxically, even after picking up this hefty price tag, the female and male Black bodies remain an uncomfortable presence in academies of the Global North. They need to be put in their place. They are constantly helped to remember that contraction is the model of accommodation assigned to them, and that White rage is elicited when these conditions are breached. 'The trigger for White rage', writes Carol Anderson (2016: 9), 'is black advancement... blackness with ambition, with drive, with purpose, with aspirations, and with demands for full and equal citizenship'. Academic citizenship would be the case here. To test and punish the resolve of the Black body, to deny full academic citizenship to a Black body that is keen on making it to the professoriate, an armada of insidious schemes is crafted.

Experiences of life under these conditions have been recently documented in a 2019 collection, *Black Academic Voices: The South African Experience*, authored by a group of mainly Black female academics. In the volume, edited by Grace Khunou and others, these scholars articulate their struggles in a male and White dominated academy that has in place schemes to contain Blackness. The titles of several of the chapters are instructive of establishment responses to the Black female presence: *Negotiating the academy: Black bodies 'out of place'*; *'Writing to stay: Running shoes replaced with high heels'*; *'Intellectual and emotional toxicity: where a cure does not appear to be imminent'*; *'Thinking while Black'*; *'Black and foreign: Negotiating being different in South Africa's academy'*; and *'Sitting on one bum: The struggle of survival and belonging for a Black woman in the academy'*. Unchained, these voices have refused to be silenced any further.

(7) A final talking point to be highlighted here has to do with a set of dimensions of knowledge production. It is a trite point that education and knowledge are relevant for development. This is the case in at least two senses: an instrumentalist/service provider sense and a fundamental sense of engine of development, that is, catalytic of innovation and research and development (R&D) (Cloete & Maassen, 2017). The passionate argument in the current volume about the role of language in education for/and development is well founded. Without essentialising the link between language and R&D, it is unsurprising that Africa and Asia, which have traditionally had different approaches to language policy in education, have very different score cards in terms of relevant parameters, for example, research output, the percentage of national populations engaged in research and development, and so on. Asia's more widespread use of national languages in (higher) education has clearly paid off. Africa is one continent where education can be delivered, from primary to tertiary levels, in a language that alienates the very people the education is intended to include and serve.

Considering the academy's mandate in knowledge production, it would seem self-defeating for it to allow sexism (as an instance of monoculture of classification) and prejudice against knowledge genres (monoculture of knowledge) to restrict the pool and quality of publicly available knowledge. The book draws attention to the low status accorded knowledge produced by women (e.g. in politics and in sociolinguistics). The example is cited of Amy Ashwood Garvey, the wife of Marcus Garvey, whose journalistic writings and public (speaking) engagements probably had greater impact on the United Negro Improvement Association and on the pan-Africanist movement than her husband's more philosophical writings. Yet, compared to her husband, she is much less well known, if at all, in political theory. Practice, her own theory, was not written down in the highfalutin jargon characteristic of theory.

This volume's treatment of the bias of gender and the bias of genre in scholarship calls to mind work in other areas. The fabricated nonexistence of women in some key writings on African history has been noted by African feminist, Amina Mama (2018). She underscores the observation by Paul Zeleza that women are not included as (chapter) authors in, let alone editors of, the eight-volume UNESCO *General History of Africa*. In several of these volumes, as in another influential collection, women are hardly present, not even as subject. *Epistemological femicide* might be coined to designate this fabricated nonexistence of women in Africa's past.

In respect of knowledge and textual genres, Ernest Boyer and Clifford Geertz may be enlisted to accentuate the corresponding points in the book. Boyer has argued for a more capacious understanding of scholarship, one that transcends research. Boyer's notion of the *scholarship of engagement* is knowledge production that arises from reciprocal links between community activism/civic advocacy and four other notions of scholarship, namely, *research, teaching, integration, and application* – which, by the way, are reciprocally influencing (Boyer, 1990; Barker, 2004). For Clifford Geertz, a postmodern *refiguration*, that is, the transcending of disciplinary boundaries, not unlike Gordon's teleological suspension of disciplinarity, calls for the blurring of genres, which may easily see:

philosophical inquiries looking like literary criticism (think of Stanley Cavell on Beckett or Thoreau, Sartre on Flaubert), scientific discussions looking like belles lettres morceaux (Lewis Thomas, Loren Eisley), baroque fantasies presented as deadpan empirical observations (Borges, Barthelme), histories that consist of equations and tables or law court testimony (Fogel and Engerman, Le Roi Ladurie), ... methodological polemics got up as personal memoirs (James Watson). Nabokov's *Pale Fire*, that impossible object made of poetry and fiction, footnotes and images from the clinic, seems very much of the time; one waits only for quantum theory in verse or biography in algebra. (Geertz, 1980: 165–166)

So, where does this all lead? I wish to conclude this epilogue with three points. First, as both a call and a response, this volume and the conversation series from which it arises are easily linked to a quote attributed to the Nigerian novelist, Chinua Achebe: 'If you don't like someone's story, write your own'. Second, I would like to suggest that this volume underscores the need to bring historical acuity to readings and analyses of coloniality as experience. Third, I might suggest that the standards for judging this volume, others that are forthcoming and the conversation series itself, will have to be expressed interrogatively as follows: talking the talk alone or walking the walk as well? To borrow from Marshall McLuhan, in this and future volumes, is and will the medium also be the message? The message, as has been argued all along, has to be one of ecologies, not of monocultures.

## References

Andersen, C.H. (n.d.) *The Ugly Duckling*. https://reader.activelylearn.com/authoring/preview/758014/notes

Anderson, C. (2016) *White Rage: The Unspoken Truth of Our Racial Divide*. New York: Bloomsbury.

Antia, B.E. (2007) LSP Studies: Factoring in indeterminacy. In B.E. Antia (ed.) *Indeterminacy in Terminology and LSP* (pp. xi–xx). Amsterdam/Philadelphia: John Benjamins.

Antia, B.E. and van der Merwe, C. (2019) Speaking with a forked tongue about multilingualism in the language policy of a South African university. *Language Policy* 18 (3), 407–429.

Barker, D. (2004) The scholarship of engagement: A taxonomy of five emerging practices. *Journal of Higher Education Outreach and Engagement* 9 (2), 123–137.

Boyer, E.L. (1990) *Scholarship Reconsidered: Priorities of the Professoriate*. New York: Carnegie Foundation for the Advancement of Teaching.

Brann, C.M.B. (1980) *Mother Tongue, Other Tongue and Further Tongue. The Triglottic Configuration in Nigeria*. Inaugural lecture, University of Maiduguri Press. Republished under the same title as Chapter 1 of C.M.B. Brann (with the assistance of Baba Mai Bello), *Language in Education and Society: An Anthology of Selected Writings of C.M.B. Brann (1975–2005)*. Maiduguri: Library of Language in Education and Society, University of Maiduguri, 2006.

Chinweizu, I. (1975) *The West and the Rest of Us*. New York: Vintage Books (a division of Random House).

Cloete, N. and Maassen, P. (2017) Roles of universities and the African context. In J. Muller, N. Cloete and F. van Schalkwyk (eds) *Castells in Africa: Universities and Development* (pp. 95–112). Cape Town: African Minds.

Flores, N. and Rosa, J. (2015) Undoing appropriateness: Raciolinguistic ideologies and language diversity in education. *Harvard Educational Review* 85 (2), 149–301.

Geertz, C. (1980) Blurred genres: The refiguration of social thought. *The American Scholar* 49 (2), 165–179.

Gordon, L.R. (2021) *Freedom, Justice, and Decolonization*. New York: Routledge.

Halliday, M.A.K. and Martin, J.R. (1993) *Writing Science: Literacy and Discursive Power.* London: The Falmer Press.

Khunou, G., Phaswana, E.D., Khooza-Shangase, K. and Canham, H. (2019) *Black Academic Voices: The South African Experience.* Cape Town: HSRC Press.

Laye, C. (1959) *The African Child* (Translated by James Kirkup). Glasgow: Fontana Books.

Makoni, S. (2003) From misinvention to disinvention of language: Multilingualism and the South African Constitution. In S. Makoni, G. Smitherman, A. Spears and A. Ball (eds) *Black Linguistics: Language, Society and Politics in Africa and the Americas* (pp. 132–151). London: Routledge.

Makoni, S. and Pennycook, A. (2005) Disinventing and reconstituting languages. *Critical Inquiry in Language Studies* 2 (3), 137–156.

Mama, A. (2018) *Undoing Pacification: Memory, Her(his)story and Feminist African Emergence* [Workshop presentation]. African Feminist History Workshop. African Feminist Initiative, Pennsylvania State University, University Park, PA.

Mazrui, A.A. (1978) *Political Values and the Educated Class in Africa.* London: Heinemann.

Mignolo, W.D. (2011) *The Darker Side of Western Modernity: Global Futures, Decolonial Options.* Durham, NC: Duke University Press.

Nkrumah, K. (1969) *Axioms of Kwame Nkrumah: Freedom Fighters' Edition.* London: Panaf Books.

Olive Network (n.d.) Ubuntu: I am because we are. https://olivenetwork.org/Issue/ubuntu-i-am-because-we-are/24347

de Sousa Santos, B. (2016) *Epistemologies of the South: Justice against Epistemicide.* New York: Routledge.

# Index

*Note:* 'n' refers to chapter notes.

Abdelhay, A. 2, 41, 42–3, 44, 45
Aboriginal peoples *see also* Indigenous
        peoples
    New Zealand 80, 82
    South America 19–20, 22
academia *see also* universities
    Black academics 56–7, 75, 105, 106, 107
    Black female scholars 55–7, 72, 75, 106, 107
    casualization of ix
    changes in ix
    decolonizing 13–23, 73, 100, 101, 105–7
    internationalization 105–6
    local situation of universities 14–15, 105
    misrecognition and microaggressions 9
    UK versus US 74
academic freedom 105
accents 85–6, 88, 93
Achebe, C. 108
African history, lack of female scholars in 107
African languages 20, 21, 32, 33
African philosophy 4, 7, 98, 103
African sociolinguistics 6–7
African Studies Global Forum (ASGF) 1–2, 99
African universities 14, 15, 105
Afrikaans 20–1, 22, 93, 97
AILA (International Association of Applied
        Linguistics) 2
Ainu 22
Ahmed, S. 50
Ajayi, J.F. 105
Alemannus, Everardus 103
Alexander, N. 97
alternative normatives 6
Andersen, C.H. 98
Anderson, C. 106
Anishinaabe 56, 59
Anishinaabek 59
anthropology 31, 45, 52, 80, 98
Antia, B. 2, 24, 75, 101, 103

    personal vignette 9–10
anti-colonial movements 3, 38, 68, 100
anti-oppressive education 58, 60–1
anti-racism work 48, 49, 53, 72
#AnYeYiYang 4
Anzaldúa, G. 8
apartheid 5, 17, 33, 93
applied linguistics 26, 30, 32, 44, 75
Arabic (Quranic) 34
Arabic (Standard) 41
Arabic linguistics 41, 43
Arabization 18–19
Arendt, H. 49
Asia x, 5, 16, 23, 35, 107
Austin, J. 91
Australia 5
authority 26
authorship and theory 72

Bagga-Gupta, S. 35–6
Bahasa 21, 22
Baker, J. 37, 38
Bangladesh 61–2
Baugh, J. 2, 84–97, 100
Bauman, R. 42
'Behind the Rhodes statue: Black competency
        and the imperial academy' (Shilliam,
        2019) 2, 68–83, 100
Bell, A. 38
Berlant, L. 50
*Beyond the Colour Line* (Prah, 1998) 17
Bhambra, G.K. 3, 4, 71
Bible 27, 40, 86
bilingualism 44 *see also* multilingualism;
        translanguaging
Black academics 56–7, 75, 105, 106, 107
Black bodies 68–83, 106
'Black Bodies' (poem) 70
Black cognitive competency 69, 71, 106

Black Lives Matter 3, 4–5, 18, 31, 32, 73, 75, 92
Black Studies 75, 76
Black women and #MeToo 4
Black women scholars 55–7, 72, 75, 106, 107
Blommaert, J. ix
Blyden, E.W. 105
bomb threats 89–90
'book,' decolonization of the 6
borders 8
Bourdieu, P. 62
Boyer, E. 107
brain development 37–8
Brazil 2, 8, 22, 54, 58, 77, 94–6
Brazilian Portuguese 22
Briggs, C. 42
Bright, W. 53
Bulgaria 5

Calvente, A. 57–8
Canada 24, 48, 50, 52, 53, 56, 60, 61, 64, 65
Canagarajah, S. 44
Cantonese 37, 43
capitalism 7, 18, 30, 48, 52–4, 58, 60, 61, 99
care, circles of 60
Caribbean 53, 59
Casley-Hayford, J.E. 105
caste systems 17
casualisation of academia ix
Centre for Advanced Studies of African
    Society (CASAS) 100
Challenge of Decolonizing Education (Prah,
    2018) 2, 13–23, 100
Chandra, G. 4
China 4, 22, 31, 33, 40, 42
Chinweizu, I. 105
ch'ixi 8
Chomskyan 25, 28, 30
Christianity 39, 71
citation
    of Black scholars 55–7, 80
    of Indigenous peoples 54
    politics of 49, 51
    of scholars accused of sexual harassment
        4, 55
    of women 55–7
citizenship 17, 42, 62, 106
classics 73, 105, 106
Cloete, N. 107
Coetzee-Van Rooy, S. 20, 36, 45, 81
cognitive processes 31, 71, 106
Cohen, M. 94
collegiality ix–x

colonialism
    and Black cognitive competency 71
    Canada 60
    colonizers' languages 19
    decolonization not limited to areas with a
        history of 3
    education 81–2
    and linguistics 30
    and nationalism 42
    neocolonialism 16, 23
    settler colonialism 3, 16, 18, 48, 53,
        54, 73
    universities in Africa 14
Comaroff, J. 3
commodification ix, 59, 62, 103
Commons 58, 59, 104
Commonwealth 74–5
community gardens 60
conferences, cost of ix, 2
Connell, R. ix, 54
contact zones 8
'core language' clusters 20, 21
COVID-19
    academic funding cuts 75
    food security/food sovereignty 60–1
    as global context for ASGF 3
    inequality ix–x
    as one of multiple crises 49
    online teaching 49
    tribalisms and populisms 5–6
creoles 53, 59
critiques of decolonial lens 3–4
culture
    cultural change 17–18
    cultural spaces 19
    and literacy 23
    recognition of cultural differences 19
curriculum 13–14, 69, 75, 81, 105, 106
Cusicanqui, S. 8

Davis, A. 50
Davis, C. 84–5
De Fina, A. 44
Decentering the Anglosphere 57
decolonial linguistics, definition x–xi
Decolonizing Politics (Shilliam, 2021) 68
definition of decolonialization 2–4
dehumanizing 5, 70, 79
democracy 18, 19, 23, 63, 96
'denigatory Blackness' 69
depoliticization of linguistics 42–3
Descola, P. 1

Dewey, W. 78
Diagne, S.B. 5, 6
Diaz, J. 49, 50
dictionaries 33, 43
diglossia 43
discourse analysis 85
displaced persons 3, 7
diversity and inclusion 10, 73–4, 79–80, 81, 96
Dixon, R.A.W. 34
'dog whistles' 91, 94
DuBois, W.E.B. 73
Duncker, D. 39

early child literacy 37
Eastern Europe 3, 4
economics 58, 68
editors of journals 57
education see also academia; universities
   anti-oppressive education 58, 60–1
   colonialism in 81–2
   curriculum 13–14, 69, 81, 105, 106
   for/and development 107
   diversity and inclusion 107
   ideology 62–3
   importance of language in decolonizing
      education 19
   and language ideologies 44, 45
   language policy 107
   multilingualism in 20
   reimagining 64
   sociology of 62
Ekotto, F. 5
elites 14, 16, 17
embodiment 64
#EndSARS 5
English
   in academia 38
   in Africa 16, 21
   anti-oppressive education 62
   in Hong Kong 38
   and knowledge production 22
   language ideologies 28, 32
   in South Africa 96–7
environmental justice 48
epidermalization of inferiority 9
Erlingsdottir, I. 4
Ethiopianism 68
ethnocide 22
ethnography 56
Eurocentrism 3, 4, 7, 69
European romanticism 34, 36–7

exclusion x, 60, 66, 74, 79, 103
experts, assumptions of the 45

Fanon, F. 9
fascism x, 17, 30, 38, 50, 68, 72, 103
father-tongue concepts 35–6, 37, 103
#FeesMustFall 2–3
feminist scholarship 55, 107
Ferguson, A. 71
Ferguson, C. 43
Figueiredo, E.H.D. x
Fishman, J. 30, 34, 39
Flores, N. 91–2, 104
Floyd, George 5, 83n(1), 104–5
folk ideologies 43, 44, 45
food security/food sovereignty 59, 60–1
forensic linguistics 84–97, 100
Foucault, M. 72
Freire, P. 6
French 16, 17, 20, 23

García, O. xi, 44, 45, 91–2
gardens 60
Garvey, A.A. 72, 107
Garvey, M. 72, 107
Garza, A. 5
gated communities 60
Geertz, C. 107
gender see also women
   disaggregation of research output by 106
   Gender Studies 75
   gender-based violence 4
   inequities x, 8
   mother-tongue concepts 103
   fabricated nonexistence 107
   rethinking theory 72
genre bias 6, 107–8
Global Blackness 5
Global South x, 2, 3, 5–9, 24, 54, 99, 105
good person, reimagining a 65
Gordon, J. 5
Gordon, L.R. 99, 104, 107
Gramsci, A. 61
Great Lakes 48, 56, 59
Gumperz, J. 53, 56, 61

Halliday, M.A.K. 103
Hansen, K. 2
Happy Valley 69
Harney, S. 50
Harris, R. 24, 25–6, 31, 32–3, 41, 42, 100

Hawai'i 53, 60
Hebrew (Modern) 21, 22, 36–7
Hegel, G.W.F. 15
hegemonic knowledges 99
Heller, M. 1, 2, 4, 24, 48–67, 100
Herder, J.G. 35
hierarchies 34, 44, 60, 101, 103
Hindi 22
Holmwood, J. 4
Hong Kong 31–3, 37, 38
hope xi, 48–50, 51, 64
Horner, B. 44
Horton, J.A. 105
Horton, M. 6
Hutton, C. 2, 24–47, 100
Hymes, D. 4, 49, 50, 51, 55, 56

Idem, U. 36, 69–71, 74
ideology
    in Arabic linguistics 43
    education and language ideologies 44, 45
    educational ideology 62–3
    English language 28, 32
    folk ideologies 43, 44, 45
    of Global South 99
    linguistics 28, 31, 43
    monolingual ideologies 20, 37, 46, 96
    mother-tongue ideologies 29, 33–4
    native speaker ideologies 28, 32, 33–4, 39,
        41, 102
    raciolinguistics 92
    and 'translanguaging' 41, 43
Igono, J. 96
imagery 78
inclusion and diversity 73–4, 79–80, 81, 96
India 22, 53, 61, 63
Indigenous languages 40, 54, 59, 62, 64, 97
Indigenous peoples
    and the American academy 54
    Australia 5
    Canada 64
    education 64
    indigenous movements 5
    mother-tongue concepts 39
    Native Americans 19, 40, 93
    New Zealand 80, 82
    South America 19–20, 22
    theoretical perspectives from 56
    United States 93
    and water 56, 58, 59
inequality ix–x, 2, 5, 9, 10, 51, 52, 81, 95, 102

Ingold, T. 1
institutional history of ideas 31
integrationism 34
intellectual history 24, 25, 27, 29–30, 51, 100, 103
intentionality 91, 95
interconnectivity 61
interdisciplinary concepts 44, 58, 94
intergenerational platforms 4, 81
International African Service Bureau 72
international conferences, cost of ix, 2
intersectionality x, 8, 93
inter-species communication 7, 59, 103–4
interstices 63
intuition 28, 32
Ireland 22
Italy 63

Jacobs, M. 54
Japan 15, 22
Jesuits 40
Jewish communities 36–7, 54
Jones, P. 39
Joseph, J. 103
Journal of Sociolinguistics 57
journals 57

Kaiper-Marquez, A. 1
Kanavillil Rajagopalan 32, 90–1, 97
Karkov, N. 3, 5
Kenya 81
Khunou, G. 106
KiSwahili 20
Klein, N. 50
Kloss, H. 29–30, 39
knowledge
    and the academy 107
    common-sense 103
    ecologies of knowledge 102–3, 106, 108
    ethics of 99
    hegemonic knowledges 99
    Indigenous knowledge systems 80
    knowledge production 22–3, 65, 69, 107
    and language 22–3
    living knowledge traditions 72, 80
    local knowledge 14–15, 105
    monocultures of 101
    nonexistent knowledge 101
    reclamation 56
    and social justice 74
    universal knowledge 21–2, 23
Kohn, E. 1

Labov, W. 56, 61
land 4, 7, 19, 40, 54–61, 64, 76, 79
language
    African languages and decolonization
        16–17
    and authority 26
    and communication 35, 36
    'core language' clusters 20, 21
    decolonizing education 19
    definition of a 'language' 20, 21, 22, 25, 34,
        35, 36
language (*Continued*)
    essentialisation 39, 40
    father-tongue concepts 35–6, 37, 103
    as ideological construct 45
    and knowledge production 22–3
    'language doesn't exist' 41
    language ecologies 21–2
    language myth 25–6, 42, 45
    languages as autonomous entities 25
    liberatory ideas of language 64
    linguistic repertoires/language resources 62,
        81, 102
    meta-language 38–9, 41, 45, 61, 103
    modernist concepts of 41
    mother-tongue concepts 29, 33–4, 35–6,
        37–41, 43, 102, 103
    national language status 22, 37
    nationhood and language 27, 41, 42
    neocolonialism 16
    official languages 19, 22, 23, 96, 97
    radically contextual nature of 32–3
    as record of history 22
    repressive notions of 52
    and social life 61
    socio-political concepts of 25
    standardized varieties of languages 21, 33
    varieties of languages 20, 21, 42, 62, 63,
        85, 93
*Language, Capitalism, Colonialism*
    (Heller and McElhinny, 2017)
    2, 24, 48, 100
language planning and policy 29–30, 31, 35,
    62, 97, 107 *see also* national language
    status; official languages
*Language Policy* 10, 57
language rights 10, 29
language testing 33
lateral thinking 25, 100, 103
Latin 38, 39, 40
Latin America 16, 19, 95

law 24–47
Laye, C. 103–4
lazy reason 99, 101
Lear, J. 50
Lee, E. 44, 46
legal purposes, linguistics for 84–97
lexicography 33, 43
liberal arts 73
liberal education 74
liberalism 38
liberatory ideas of language 64
linguistic market 62
linguistic profiling 84–9, 94
linguistic repertoires/language resources 62,
    81, 102
linguistics
    applied linguistics 26, 30, 32, 44, 75
    and Black Lives Matter 31
    depoliticization of 42–3
    as discipline 25, 27, 28, 30, 32, 41–2
    for legal purposes 84–97
    malleability of 30
    non-human linguistics 7, 59, 104
    and North America 53
    and race 27–8, 31, 93
    stuck in 19th century 32–3
    Western linguistics traditions 25, 43
*Linguistics and the Third Reich* (Hutton,
    1999) 2, 24–47, 100
*Linguistics in Pursuit of Justice* (Baugh, 2018)
    2, 84–97, 100
listservs 2
literacy 20, 23, 26, 37–8, 44, 96
living knowledge traditions 72, 80
local elites 16
local knowledge 14–15, 21, 105
locus of enunciation 8, 65
Lomeu Gomes, R. xi, 1, 2, 48, 66, 68, 74, 79,
    80, 84, 90
    personal vignette 8

Maassen, P. 107
Madany-Saá, M. 1, 2, 19, 20, 21, 31, 33, 35,
    44, 46
    personal vignette 7–8
Makoni, B. 55, 57, 79
Makoni, S. xi, 1, 2, 4, 13, 14, 16, 17, 18, 24–5,
    26, 27, 28, 29–30, 32, 33, 34, 35–6, 39,
    51, 52, 53, 54, 56, 58, 64, 66, 68, 69, 70,
    71, 72–3, 74, 75, 82, 84, 90, 99, 103
    personal vignette 6–7

Maldonado-Torres, N. 4
Malinowski, B. 71
Mama, A. 107
Mamdani, M. 3
Mandamin, J. 56
Māori people 80, 82
Martin, J.R. 103
Martin, Trayvon 4–5
Martinez, J. x
Martin-Jones, M. 63
Mazrui, A. 105
Mbembe, A. 3
McElhinny, B. 1, 2, 4, 24, 48–67, 100
McLuhan, M. 108
meaning-making practices 41, 52
media 63
medicine 94
Memmi, A. 69
Mesthrie, R. 97
meta-language 38–9, 41, 45, 61, 103
metaphors 3, 58, 59, 60, 61, 104
metonymic reason 101, 102
#MeToo 3, 4, 5
metropolitanism 16
microaggressions 9, 70
Mignolo, W. xi, 1, 11, 66, 99
Milojicic, V. 2
minorities 17–18, 19, 23, 31, 86, 94
misrecognition 9
missionaries 30, 34, 40
Mitchell-Kernan, C. 55–6, 57
modernism 41
Mogstad, H. 3
monocultures 101–2, 103, 106, 107
monolingual ideologies 20, 37, 46, 96
Morgan, M. 55–6
Moten, F. 50
mother-tongue concepts 29, 33–4, 35–6,
    37–41, 43, 102, 103
Mufwene, S. x
Mühlhäusler, P. 34
multiculturalism 60
multilingualism
    in Africa 20, 33, 96–7
    and monolingual ideologies 46
    multilingual language policies 19–20
    multilingual pedagogy 20, 81
    multilingual turn 102
    oral versus literate 20
    positionality 44
    South Africa 33, 96–7

and translanguaging 44
    urban areas 20
multispecies communication 7, 59, 103–4
Muñoz, J. 50

naming 39, 78–9
narratives 51, 56, 63, 64, 99
national language status 22, 37
nationalism 29, 31, 37, 42, 48, 72, 76
nationhood and language 27, 41, 42
Native Americans 19, 40
native speaker ideologies 28, 32, 33–4, 39,
    41, 102
natural language processing 28
Nazi Germany 24–47, 103
Ndlangamandla, S. 1, 96
neocolonialism 16, 23
Nestlé 58–9
New Zealand 80, 82
Nigeria 5, 96, 99, 100, 103
Nkrumah, K. 105
Noah, T. 10
nonexistence 101, 104, 107
non-human linguistics 7, 59, 103–4
Northern Ireland 18

Oduor, J. 81
Odugu, D. 1
official languages 19, 22, 23, 96, 97
Omoniyi, T. 75
On Decoloniality (Mignolo and Walsh, 2018)
    1, 66
one-language-nation-state 102
online collegiality x
ontological visibility 77
orality 20, 23
Orientalism 56
orthography 20, 21, 39
Otheguy, R. 44, 45
Ottoman Empire 42
Owens, J. 43
Oxford 10, 14, 25, 33, 41, 74, 75, 76, 78, 79

Pacific societies 34
Paiter Suruí 57
Pan Africanism 17, 72, 76, 105, 107
Passeron, J.-C. 62
Pennycook, A. xi, 1, 51, 66, 103
Pérez Milans, M. 57
periphery, coming from the 56
phonetics 53, 84, 102

pidgins 53, 59
place-based approaches 59
poetry 70
police brutality 5
political economy 53, 68, 71
political issues 24–47
populisms 5
Portuguese
  in Africa 16
  in Brazil 22
positionality 44, 46, 61, 99
positivism 58, 103, 104
postcolonial contexts 16, 27, 30, 34, 38, 39,
    40, 74, 75
power
  and authority 26
  competent wielding of 65
  decolonizing the academy 73
  dominant languages 97
  and elites 16
  hegemonic knowledges 99
  and intentionality of racial slurs 91
  and language 23
  language ecologies 21–2
  and meaning-making processes 52
  metonymic reason 101
  monocultures 103
  and ontological invisibility 77
  pyramid of tyrannies 69
  and sociolinguistics 55
  translanguaging 41
  and 'universal' knowledge 21–2
  within universities 66
  White as metaphor for 104
Prah, K. 2, 3, 13–23, 100
Pratt, M.L. 8
pre-colonial languages 22, 33, 34, 40
pre-reading 2
psycholinguistics 28, 31, 37
publication of work 72, 80 see also citation
Pulaar 21
Purnell, T. 86
pyramid of tyrannies 69

Quranic Arabic 34
Qwabe, N. 79

race
  Black bodies 68–83, 106
  concepts of 17
  and linguistics 27–8, 31, 93

  and the police 85
  and politics of nonexistence 104
race theory 24, 26–7, 31
racial profiling 94
racial slurs 88–9, 90, 91
racialism 69
raciolinguistics 92
racism
  anti-Asian racism x, 5
  anti-Black racism 5, 54, 65
  Black Lives Matter 5
  Canada 60
  in courtrooms 88, 91
  COVID-19 x
  'denigatory Blackness' 69
  as effect of colonialism 95
  hopes 64
  in housing access 85–6, 94
  linguistic profiling 88–9
  and linguistics 27–8, 31
  systemic racism ix, 18, 95
  United States 18, 94, 95, 96
radical hope 48–50, 64
ranking systems 105–6
reason, shifting the geography of 99
Recollet, K. 50
refiguration of disciplinarity 107
reflexive turn 65
Reformation 38, 40, 42
reimagining what human is 56
Renzi, A. 63
research and development (R&D) 107
Research Network Africa (REN) 2
rhizomes 57–8, 59, 61, 104
Rhodes Must Fall 2–3, 75, 76, 78, 79
#RiceBunny 4
right-wing politics 29
Romania 4, 29
Rosa, J. 91–2, 94, 104
Rudwick, S. 92–3
Russia 19, 31

Said, E. 56, 59
Saint Lawrence Seaway 56
Sami people 19
Sanskrit 53
Saussure, F. de 30
scholarship of engagement 107
Scotland 18
second language acquisition 31, 32, 36, 88
Second World War 15, 27

semiotic resources 44
sense-making 9
September 11 89
settler colonialism 3, 16, 18, 19, 48, 53, 54,
      73, 75
Severo, C. 2, 39–40
sexism 4, 50, 56, 64, 99, 107
sexual harassment 4, 49, 50
Shibboleth 86
Shilliam, R. 2, 3, 68–83, 100
Shor, I. 6
Shuy, R. 84, 85
silenced voices 51, 52, 53
Simpson, L. 50
slang 43
slavery 5, 8, 18–19, 68, 95, 99
Smith, A. 71
social class x, 6, 8, 32, 56, 60, 72, 96
social conservatism 68
social justice 3, 10, 30, 45, 48, 73–4, 77,
      96, 104
social media 43, 64
Social Science Research Council Committee
      on Sociolinguistics 57
socialism 3, 56
sociolinguistics 6–7, 8, 24, 30, 32, 48–67,
      92, 100
sociology of education 62
solidarity 54, 60, 65, 66, 98
de Sousa Santos, B. 2, 12, 99, 101, 102
South Africa 3, 13, 15, 21, 24, 36, 75–80, 81,
      93, 95, 96–7, 100–1
Southern Theory 8, 26, 34, 45, 54
South-South anti-colonial connections 68
de Souza, L.M.T.M. 1, 2, 21–2, 66, 77–8, 79,
      94–5, 99, 101
Soyinka, W. xi, 10, 12, 90
Spanish 22
spectrography 87
speech act theory 91
spelling systems 20, 21
Standard Arabic 41
standardized varieties of languages 21, 33
statues xi, 11, 75, 76, 79
stereotypes 69, 70, 92
Sterling, C. 68–9, 73, 83
style shifting 85–6
Suárez-Krabbe, J. 3, 12
subaltern experiences 9, 54
Sudan 18–19, 100
Suleiman, Y. 43

Sultana, S. 61, 63, 82
Sydney Forum 1
syllabus decolonization 81 *see also* curriculum
symbolism 78, 79
systemic racism ix, 18, 95

Taiwo, O. 4
'talking books'/'conversational books' 6
Te Reo 82
teleological suspension of disciplinarity 99,
      104, 107
textbook format 52
theology 39–40
theory 71–2, 73, 99, 107
*Theory from the South* (Comaroff and
      Comaroff, 2011) 3
transcription xii, 6, 39, 84
transdisciplinary approaches 7, 58
translanguaging 26, 37–9, 41, 42–3, 44,
      45, 46
tribalisms 5
Trump, D. 8, 50, 67, 94, 95
Tse, L. 3
Tuck, E. 4, 12

ubuntu 11, 98, 109
Uighurs 22
ultimate attainment 31, 32
United Kingdom
   academia 74–5
   calls for decolonization 3
   colonialism 56, 74–5
   Rhodes Must Fall 76, 79
   and Scotland 18
United States
   American academy 53–4, 74–5
   apartheid 93
   BLM protests, 83
   calls for decolonization 3
   as default place 25, 28
   election/politics 50
   election/politics & racism, 91
   Empire of 53
   global dominance 27
   Indigenous peoples 19, 40, 93
   medical care 94
   multilingualism 97
   Native Americans 19, 40
   personal bio 52
   personal intro 3, 4, 5, 48
   policing/law 85, 86, 88

racial discrimination 18
racism 18, 94, 95, 96
Rhodes Must Fall 76, 78
sociolonguistics 56
universal ideas 14, 15, 22, 101, 103
universal knowledge 21–2, 23
Universal Negro Improvement Association
    (UNIA) 72, 107
universalism xi, 14, 30, 34, 101–2
universities xi, 100, 108
    African universities xi, 13–23, 80, 81, 105,
        106
    Black staff 66
    Black students 76
    Brazil 77
    building non-colonial 105
    colonial heritage 74–5, 105
    decolonization 3, 13–23, 72, 73
    elites 14, 16
    Indigenous knowledge systems 80
    internationalization 105–6
    Kenya 81–2
    and politics of nonexistence 105
    segregationist institutions 73, 76

van der Merwe, C. i, vii, 2, 101
van Pinxteren, B. 21
varieties of languages 20, 21, 42, 62, 63,
    85, 93
Verfaille, J. vii, xi, 1–2
Vietnam 31
viewpoints of history 15
virtual communication 49
virtual reading group 1
*Volk* 27, 29, 37, 42, 46

Wa Thiong'o, Ngugi 4, 82, 105
walking backwards into the future 56, 61–2

Walsh, C. xi, xii, 1, 11, 12, 66, 67
Washington, B. T. 73
water xi, 28, 48, 54, 55, 56, 58–9, 64, 70, 104
Weinreich, U. 30, 47
Weisgerber, L. 29, 30, 37
Weldon, T. 85
Western linguistics traditions 24, 43
white listening subjects 91, 92, 104–5
white male domination 106
white male heteronormativity 4
White rage 106, 108
White supremacy 5, 26–7, 30
Williams, R. 56
Wiredu, K. 4
wiretapping 85, 86–7
women x, 4–5, 10, 48, 56
    #MeToo 4
    access to scholarship 81
    Black female scholars 55–7, 72, 75,
        106, 107
    citation of 55–7
    education by missionaries 40
    fabricated nonexistence 107
    gender and Pan Africanism 72
    theoretical perspectives from 56
Woodward, B. 95
World Bank 57–8
World Englishes 33
#WoYeShi 4
writing, definitions of 26
Wynter, S. 50, 56, 71

xenophobia 26–7

Yang, K.W. 4, 24

Zeleza, P. 3, 107, 119
Zoom x